CULTURES OF THE WORLD®

AFGHANISTAN

Sharifah Enayat Ali

MARSHALL CAVENDISH BENCHMARK

NEW YORK

PICTURE CREDITS

Cover photo: © Adam Buchanan / Danita Delimont Stock Photography

AFP: 30 • alt.TYPE / Reuters: 17, 29, 33, 35, 40, 42, 90, 114, 115, 119, 124 • AP Photo / Noor Khan: 38 • Audrius Tomonis: 135 • Focus Team: 68, 96, 99 • HBL Network Photo Agency: 1, 5, 6, 16, 31, 32, 34, 37, 50, 51, 55, 56, 57, 58, 59, 60, 76, 78, 100, 109, 112, 122, 123, 128 • Hutchison: 61, 65, 66, 69, 71, 80, 87, 89, 92, 95, 105, 111, 127 • Life File Photos Ltd: 12, 21, 45, 64, 103, 104 • Lonely Planet Images: 27, 53, 54, 102, 110, 116, 129 • MCIA—Mabelle Yeo & Bernard Go: 130 • Photobank / Photolibrary: 7, 9, 11, 85 • Pietro Scozarri: 22 • Stockfood: 131 • The Image Bank: 3, 4, 13, 14, 41, 47, 63, 73, 108 • Yeo Chong Jin: 125

PRECEDING PAGE

A group of rural Afghan children in colorful clothes stand in a field at the foot of the vast and imposing Hindu Kush.

Editorial Director (U.S.): Michelle Bisson
Editors: Deborah Grahame, Mabelle Yeo
Copyreader: Daphne Hougham
Designers: Jailani Basari, Bernard Go Kwang Meng
Cover picture researcher: Connie Gardner
Picture researchers: Thomas Khoo, Joshua Ang

Marshall Cavendish Benchmark
99 White Plains Road
Tarrytown, NY 10591
Web site: www.marshallcavendish.us

Originated and designed by Times Editions
An imprint of Marshall Cavendish International (Asia) Private Limited
A member of Times Publishing Limited

All Internet sites were correct and accurate at the time of printing. All monetary figures in this publication are in U.S. dollars.

Library of Congress Cataloging-in-Publication Data
Ali, Sharifah Enayat, 1943–
    Afghanistan / by Sharifah Enayat Ali. — 2nd ed.
        p. cm. — (Cultures of the world)
    Summary: "Provides comprehensive information on the geography, history, governmental structure, economy, cultural
        diversity, peoples, religion, and culture of Afghanistan" — Provided by publisher.
    Includes bibliographical references and index.
        ISBN-13: 978-0-7614-2064-4
        ISBN-10: 0-7614-2064-9
    1. Afghanistan—Juvenile literature. I. Title. II. Series.
    DS351.5.A44 2006
    958.1—dc22   2005034789

Printed in China

9 8 7 6 5 4 3 2 1

CONTENTS

An Afghan youth wears a cloth around his head for protection against sandstorms whipped up by strong winds.

Centuries-old ruins such as this one lie just outside Kabul, the capital of Afghanistan since 1776.

INTRODUCTION

AFGHANISTAN, OR "LAND OF THE AFGHANS," a patchwork of diverse kingdoms, came into existence as a single entity only in the 18th century. Lying at the crossroads between Europe and the Far East, a steady stream of conquerors, adventurers, and soldiers of fortune has arrived there through the narrow passes of the Hindu Kush throughout the centuries.

The Afghans had often been called "giant killers." Both Darius I of Persia and Alexander the Great of Macedonia found them to be a formidable foe, as did, much later, the British and the Russians. However, the last two decades of the 20th century, from the Soviet occupation to the overthrow of the severe Taliban regime, left Afghanistan devastated—its farmlands were ravaged, pastures were riddled with land mines, and cities were ruined. Its environment has fallen to a critical point of disrepair. Dependent now on foreign aid in establishing the foundations for reconstruction, Afghanistan is at a turning point in its history. There is hope for the peace that has always eluded conflict-ridden Afghanistan and its people.

GEOGRAPHY

THE COUNTRY OF AFGHANISTAN lies between latitudes 29° and 38°N and longitudes 61° and 75°E in southwestern Asia. With a land area of about 250,000 square miles (647,500 sq km), it is approximately the size of Texas. Much of the country is covered by the mountain ranges of the Hindu Kush, which rise to heights of 24,000 feet (7,300 m) in the east. In addition, there are extensive deserts and plains.

Afghanistan is a landlocked country. To the north lie the Central Asian republics that once belonged to the Soviet Union—Uzbekistan, Tajikistan, and Turkmenistan. Part of the boundary with these republics, about 700 miles (1,126 km) long, is formed by the Oxus River, now called the Amu Dar'ya. To the east and southeast, separated by the Durand Line, lies Pakistan. To the west lies Iran, while the Chinese province of Sinkiang, also known as Xinjiang, borders the Wakhan Mountains in the northeast.

Almost all references in Western sources define Hindu Kush as "kills the Hindu," a grim reminder of the days when many Indians died in the high mountain passes of Afghanistan, on their way to the slave markets of Muslim Central Asia.

—Louis Dupree

Left: **Traversing the rocky and rugged terrain in central Afghanistan is a precarious task.**

Opposite: **Vast stretches of perilous mountains, arid valleys, and dry desert land add to the hot and harsh climate of Afghanistan.**

TOPOGRAPHY

Afghanistan can be divided broadly into three regions—the northern plains, the central mountains, and the southern plateau.

NORTHERN PLAINS This region has some of the most fertile land in Afghanistan and is the country's major agricultural area. Because rainfall is inadequate, however, only river valleys and regions where water is available can be cultivated.

Irrigation systems have been built along some rivers. The Kokcha and the Kunduz—two important tributaries of the Amu Dar'ya River flowing from the Hindu Kush—enable farmers to cultivate rice and cotton. Semi-nomads also raise sheep and goats on the vast grasslands here.

CENTRAL MOUNTAINS Afghanistan's mountain ranges are an extension of the Himalayan Mountains and cover about two-thirds of the country. The Hindu Kush, which extends across the country from the southeast to the northeast, forms the backbone of Afghanistan's central mountains.

The famed snowcapped Kohi Baba Mountains, which rise to almost 17,000 feet (5,182 m), make up the southwestern branch of the Hindu Kush. The highest mountain here is the Shah Fuladi (16,873 feet or 5,143 m). The tallest peaks in the country, however, are found near the northeastern border with Pakistan, where the Nowshak (24,557 feet or 7,485 m), Afghanistan's highest mountain, is located. The northeastern part of the highlands, including the Wakhan, is geologically active. In the 20th century alone, more than a dozen earthquakes occurred in the area around Kabul.

The 435-mile (700-km) Kabul River is a vital source of water here, as its tributaries irrigate some of the most productive agricultural land in the country. To the east the Khyber Pass enables travelers to traverse the daunting terrain of the Hindu Kush into Pakistan. Another mountain route, the Baroghil Pass, links the Wakhan Valley with northern Pakistan.

Afghanistan's steep and mountainous terrain renders traveling treacherous. As such, narrow pathways, or passes, made through the country's mountains are of great economic and military significance. The Khyber Pass is one of the most famous and important passes in the world, and it links Afghanistan and Pakistan. It has served as a strategic and vital trade and invasion route through history.

SOUTHERN PLATEAU The southwestern region primarily consists of desert and semidesert land. The largest deserts here are the Registan, Dashti Margo, and Dashti Khash. These barren areas, which cover over 40,000 square miles (103,600 square km), lie between 1,500 and 2,000 feet (450 and 600 m) above sea level. The entire region is bisected by the Helmand River, which flows from the Hindu Kush to Lake Helmand, a vast, marshy lake in the Sistan Basin on the Iranian border. Lake Helmand, one of the few lakes in Afghanistan, expands and contracts with the seasonal flow of its rivers. In the extreme southwest of the great plateau is the marshland of Gawd-i-Zirreh.

CLIMATE

Severe winters and long, hot summers characterize Afghanistan's climate. The weather is influenced more by its high altitude than by its latitude. From December to March air masses come from the cold north, bringing very cold weather and snow to the mountains.

Rich agricultural land near Jalalabad, east of the Hindu Kush. Agriculture is the mainstay of Afghanistan's economy. Important food crops include wheat, rice, barley, and corn.

The name Amu Dar'ya *(Amudariya) means "Mother of Rivers."*

The Helmand River is the longest river flowing entirely within Afghanistan. It is about 879 miles (1,415 km) long and, together with its tributaries, drains the whole of southern Afghanistan. The Amu Dar'ya, which forms part of the boundary between Afghanistan and the Central Asian republics, is the major river in the north. Rising in the Hindu Kush, it flows for about 1,500 miles (2,414 km) to empty into the Aral Sea in Turkmenistan.

The climate during the months from June to September is very hot and dry, although eastern Afghanistan receives some rain. Nights can be very cold, however, even in summer. Little rain falls at lower altitudes, and the plains are extremely dry. Rainfall in the country averages just 7 inches (18 cm) a year. The southwest is even more arid than the east. Strong winds, such as the *baadi sadu beest roz* (bawh-di-sah-doh-bist-ROHZ) along the Iran-Afghanistan border, commonly cause sandstorms. In the southwestern deserts the temperature difference between day and night can be very extreme. In the summer, for example, water freezes at night, despite noon temperatures of up to 120°F (49°C).

Only in areas like Kabul, which are situated at higher altitudes and are sheltered, is the climate relatively pleasant. Kabul's yearly temperature ranges between 23°F and 77°F (−5°C and 25°C).

FLORA AND FAUNA

Less than 1 percent of Afghanistan is forested. The forests thrive mainly in the mountains and include pine, cypress, oak, juniper, laurel, barberry, hazel, and wild almond. The most prized tree is the deodar, a cedar that Afghans use to build furniture and houses. Stunted pines and oaks are also much sought after by woodcutters. In spring, flowers such as the cowslip and anemone bloom in the valleys and hillsides. As summer approaches, tulips appear, followed by petunias, sunflowers, marigolds, honeysuckles, dahlias, and geraniums.

The animals in the Hindu Kush are typical of the nearby Himalayas. They include the snowcock, ibex, brown bear, snow leopard, piping hare, and the Siberian tiger. In the northern plains can be found the fauna of the steppes (level, treeless land), such as bustards and the suslik, a ground squirrel. In the western deserts thrive the creatures characteristic

of the Caspian Sea—gazelles, coursers (a type of bird), flamingos, and swallow plovers. Camels are native to the region: the single-humped Arvana dromedary is common on the plains, and the double-humped Bactrian camel is found in the mountains. Wild pigs, which the Afghans call *khooki washi*, are found in tamarisk groves.

The cheetah, leopard, mongoose, and other animals of the Indian subcontinent are found in south and eastern Afghanistan. The macaque, a type of monkey, is found in the forested areas of Nuristan, near the Pakistani border. Leopards, otters, and foxes are sometimes hunted for their pelts, which are sold to make blankets and coats.

Fish abound in the rivers. To the north of the Hindu Kush, a trout called *mawhee khaldar* can be found. Barbels and carp thrive in all the waters, as does a tasty but bony fish called *sheer mawhee*, or milkfish. Freshwater crabs and small fish, such as minnows, help to keep the streams clean.

However, the country's once abundant biodiversity is diminishing greatly due to the damaging effects of war and environmental degradation.

Few fish and avifauna can now be found in the polluted waters and degraded banks along lower Amu Dar'ya, once endowed with a wealth of flora and wildlife.

CITIES

KABUL Kabul is strategically located close to the Khyber Pass. Nestling 6,000 feet (1,828 m) above sea level on a well-sheltered plateau, Kabul is one of the highest capital cities in the world.

Bare rocky mountains rise in the south and west. Because of the altitude, Kabul's climate is not unlike that of Denver, Colorado—invigorating, with brilliant sunshine and thin, clear air. The summers are dry, but there is rain in spring and heavy snowfall in winter, when the cultural and economic center of the country is often snowbound.

This city was once full of bazaars and narrow alleys with shops selling a wide variety of merchandise, from exotic carpets to nuts, fruits, grains, and an assortment of handcrafted items and garments. The modern parts

Eighty species of doves and pigeons populate the plains and foothills of Afghanistan. Nightingales can be heard in the summer, and jays, magpies, pipits, larks, and crows are also plentiful. Falcons, eagles, and vultures are sometimes seen patrolling the skies on the lookout for prey. Many species of game birds can also be found, including the chukar partridge, with its distinctive red bill and legs. The size of a small chicken, it is hunted for food and is also bred for fighting.

Camels are bred for transportation in Afghanistan, especially by the nomadic peoples.

of the city had wide boulevards, carrying an incredible mixture of traffic: trucks, buses, jeeps, and automobiles moving alongside camels, donkeys, and horse carts laden high with a vast array of goods and passengers.

Two decades of continual war and political chaos left a trail of devastation in Kabul. Most of the city's infrastructure services, such as electricity, water, and sanitation, were destroyed, and little had been done to build new roads and to improve telecommunications in the country. Kabul's trolley bus service came to a halt in December 1992 when a civil war started. Of the 800 buses in operation then, only 108 buses remained when service was finally restored. A $23 million project to rebuild the public electric bus system was planned. In March 2006, a link for bus service between Pakistan and Afghanistan was opened.

Kabul's estimated population of 800,000 before the war swelled to more than 3 million in 2004 after the return of millions of refugees. The exodus of the rural population to the cities has exacerbated the population pressure in the city. With many homes and buildings destroyed during the recent decades of violence, there is a very severe lack of shelter. Efforts made to

For centuries, Kabul has stood in the path of great invaders, from Alexander the Great and Genghis Khan to Tamerlane and Nadir Shah.

براساس دعوت تاریخی بین مقدس اسلام از اصول برادری، صلح و عدالت اجتماعی پیروی شا ید

هموطنان مندین!

A crowded bazaar in one of the older sections of Kabul. Transactions are carried out in the local currency, the afghani.

Kandahar was a Taliban stronghold. It is through this city that timber, fur of protected animals, and narcotics are smuggled into Pakistan.

improve the living conditions of its residents have been insufficient, and many still do not have access to safe drinking water, sanitation, electricity, and other basic amenities. Pollution levels are appalling too.

Housing projects and policies have been undertaken by the new independent government, with the aid of international humanitarian organizations such as the United Nations High Commission for Refugees. Aid efforts are made to improve the poor standard of living of the people.

Among the most noticeable developments has been the resuscitation of the bazaars and street life in Kabul. Whereas the primary color in Kabul's streets was dusty gray during the period of the Taliban, colors have returned to store fronts and to the apparel of those who frequent them. The return of music and the enthusiastic bargaining of Kabulis have restored to life once dormant shops and neighborhoods.

KANDAHAR Kandahar is the capital of Kandahar Province, one of the richest provinces in Afghanistan. Fruits, such as pomegranates, and large quantities of wool are produced in the area around the city.

Kandahar was the first capital of modern Afghanistan, and it is the country's second-largest city. It has wide, cobbled main streets. Unlike Kabul, its bazaars are roomy and open. The houses have arched doorways and are made of baked bricks laid over wooden scaffolding, which is used over and over again as wood is scarce.

The city is free of winter snow and lies on the shortest air route between Europe and Asia. It has an international airport that has largely become a military facility. An excellent road, which is open in all weather, connects the city to Pakistan.

MAZARI SHAREEF Mazari Shareef is the largest city in northern Afghanistan. It is an important and strategic trading center for the north and lies just 13 miles (21 km) southwest of the Amu Dar'ya. It is best known throughout the Islamic world as one of the reputed sites of the tomb of Hazrat Ali, the son-in-law of the Prophet Muhammad.

GHAZNI Ghazni, which lies 80 miles (129 km) south of Kabul, was the resplendent capital of Sultan Mahmud, a ruler of the Ghazni dynasty, in the 11th century. Today it is an important commercial center.

HERAT Herat is situated in the Harirud Valley, a major fruit- and grain-producing area in western Afghanistan. Its proximity to Iran made it the center for Persian art and architecture during the 15th and 16th centuries. The old city is surrounded by a large moat, massive walls, and many towers. Today a modern area has grown around the walls. Herat is famous for its carpets and woolen cloth.

In the mid-1980s Herat lost almost two-thirds of its population as residents fled the war-torn city. Today Herat, located near Iran, has an influx of refugees, as does Jalalabad, which is located near the border of Pakistan. In Herat there is a wide disparity between the standards of living of its permanent residents and the refugees.

15

HISTORY

AFGHANISTAN AS WE KNOW IT today emerged as a nation in 1747. This rugged land, which lies at the crossroads between Europe and China, has a long and turbulent history of invasion and warfare.

EARLY CIVILIZATION

Archaeological finds since 1949 reveal that humans had settled in northern Afghanistan some 50,000 years ago. Historians also believe that Afghanistan may have been one of the areas where humans first domesticated animals and raised such plants as wheat and barley.

Agricultural villages that provided food to Mohenjo-Daro, Harappa, and the other great regional centers of the Indus River Valley civilizations may have been in Afghanistan.

Above: **The citadel of Alexander the Great in Herat.**

ACHAEMENID EMPIRE

The ancient land of Bactria in northern Afghanistan first appeared in recorded history in about 540 B.C., when the Persian monarch Cyrus the Great incorporated it into his Achaemenid Empire.

Darius the Great, who ruled from 522 to 486 B.C., and Xerxes, who ruled from 486 to 465 B.C., expanded the empire farther to include provinces in and around Afghanistan, creating the largest empire of the ancient world.

GREEK RULE

Alexander the Great defeated the Persians in 328 B.C. and entered the Hindu Kush a year later. After capturing Herat, he moved on to Sakastan

Opposite: **The colossal 174-foot (53-m) statues of Buddha in Bamian were built during the period when Buddhism was a primary religion in northern Afghanistan. The Taliban destroyed the statues in 2001. Since the destruction, international efforts have been made to try to reconstruct the statues. However, hopes are dim that the statues can ever be restored to their old grandeur. The remains of the statues testify to the early influence Buddhism had on the country.**

17

As a young man, from age 13 to 16, Alexander the Great of Macedonia was taught by the Athenian philosopher Aristotle.

(modern Sistan) and later marched his army into what today is Kandahar. From here he continued up the Arghandab River valley, from Ghazni across the watershed to the Kabul Valley.

In 328 B.C., Alexander led his army north through the Hindu Kush passes and spent a year conquering the lands on both sides of the Amu Dar'ya River.

After Alexander's death in 323 B.C., Bactria became part of the Seleucid Empire. Much of the land south of the Hindu Kush fell under the control of Chandragupta, who had established the Mauryan Empire in northern India. Chandragupta was later succeeded by his grandson Ashoka, who established several important religious centers in the Hindu Kush.

In 185 B.C., the large Mauryan Empire disintegrated. The Greeks in the north, who had by then established an independent Greco-Bactrian kingdom, quickly took advantage of its decline and moved south across the Hindu Kush.

When the Bactrian Empire subsequently broke up, Greek rule in Afghanistan ended. However, their influence on art and culture remained. The combination of Grecian, Mauryan, and Kushan cultures produced what is today known as Gandharan art, found in the cities and monasteries of the Kabul Valley.

SUCCESSION OF CONQUERORS

The Saka, nomadic invaders from Central Asia, pushed the Greeks out of Bactria and northwest India, occupied Sakastan, and, for a brief period, ruled the land between the Helmand River and the Persian Gulf. Then the Parthians, who controlled Iran, conquered Sakastan and made it a Parthian satrapy, or province. At its peak, the Parthian-ruled empire extended from Armenia to India.

The Parthians were later overthrown by the Kushans from across the Amu Dar'ya. By the middle of the first century A.D., the Kushans had crossed the Hindu Kush and were ruling the entire Kabul Valley, which was known as Gandhara. The Kushans controlled all the land from the lower Indus Valley to the Iranian border and from the Chinese Sinkiang Province to the Caspian and Aral seas.

Kanishka was the greatest of the Kushan emperors. During his reign, Buddhism enjoyed its greatest influence and spread to the Far East and parts of Southeast Asia. Sculpture and art also flourished and made a great impact on the cultures of Afghanistan, India, Iran, and even China. When the Kushan dynasty ended in A.D. 220, the country became fragmented.

In the third century, Ardashir founded the mighty Sassanian dynasty, which ruled over the Persian Empire for four centuries and dominated Afghanistan and Pakistan west of the Indus.

ARRIVAL OF ISLAM

The Islamic conquest of Afghanistan has become the very essence of Afghan experience and being. The Arabs defeated the Sassanids in Persia in about A.D. 642, bringing Iran under Arab control. They crossed the Amu Dar'ya in 667 and invaded Herat. By 714, Arab control of the region up to the Indus River was complete.

During the caliphate of Harun ar-Rashid of the Abbasid dynasty, Balkh became a great seat of learning. In the ninth century the Abbasids were displaced by three local kingdoms in quick succession—the Tahirids, Saffarids, and Samanids. The Saffarids were the first to unite the regions north and south of the Hindu Kush under one rule. They were instrumental in converting the remote groups to Islam and in promoting the use of Farsi (the language of Persia) among the people. The Samanids soon

The most important archaeological find in Afghanistan was made in 1963 when the French located the Greek city of Ai Khanoum, at the confluence of the Kokcha and Darya-i-Panj rivers. This is the easternmost Greek city ever discovered and consists of several complexes. The upper town has a huge citadel, and the lower town has residential and administrative buildings, including a palace, a university, a gymnasium, and a temple.

ASHOKA'S ROCK AND PILLAR OF EDICTS

Archaeological evidence confirming the truth of historical references to the lands of the Hindu Kush has grown steadily since World War II. Ashoka's rock and pillar of edicts, for example, were found in 1958 and 1963 respectively, near Kandahar. Others were found in India and Pakistan.

Ashoka became king in about 270 B.C. The many rocks and pillars of edicts were Ashoka's way of promoting the Buddhist way of nonviolent life and through them he imparted moral values and the virtue of religious tolerance to his subjects. They were very much like billboards in the United States today, except that he was advertising a way of life instead of a product.

The edicts in Afghanistan were written in Greek and Aramaic. Aramaic was the official language of the Achaemenid Empire and the main language for most of western Asia before it was replaced by Greek and local Iranian languages. It is believed that Jesus and the first Christians spoke Aramaic.

The edicts suggest that Aramaic still existed in Ashoka's time, long after the fall of the Achaemenid Empire. They also reveal the importance of the Greeks in the Afghan region, and testify to the existence of humanitarian values at the time.

overthrew the Saffarids, and a great empire that stretched from India to Baghdad was established by 920. By 943, however, this empire had begun to disintegrate. The kings had trained Turkish slaves for military and civil use. Eventually, these slaves gained influence and power over their masters.

GHAZNAWID DYNASTY

In 962 one of the king's Turkish slaves, Alptigin, overthrew his master and became the ruler of Ghazni. Thus the Ghaznawid dynasty, which brought an era of magnificence to this region, was founded. The third ruler of this dynasty, Sultan Mahmud of Ghazni, contributed tremendously to the expansion of Islam in the region and India. Besides being a great general, successfully consolidating and expanding the dynasty's territories, he was a patron of the arts and filled his capital, Ghazni, and other cities with the best intellectuals, artists, and scientists of his time. Among the intellectuals in Mahmud's court were the poet Firdawsi, scientist-historian al-Biruni, and the historian al-Utbi. Mahmud used Afghan mercenaries in his conquest of India, where they succeeded to the throne of Delhi and the command of three important principalities. They remained renowned in India for the next 300 years for their military prowess.

After Sultan Mahmud's death in 1030, the empire declined and the dynasty was finally overthrown by the Ghorids from northwestern Afghanistan, who captured and burned the splendid city of Ghazni to the ground. The Ghorids went on to conquer India and almost forgot their homeland.

The Ghazni Victory Tower was built by Mahmud of Ghazni to commemorate his military victories.

MONGOL RULE

In the 13th century Genghis Khan swept out of Central Asia with his Mongolian forces and mercilessly destroyed everything in his path. He left ruin and desolation wherever he passed.

In 1220 Genghis Khan reached the Amu Dar'ya River and destroyed Balkh and Herat. Returning from India, he ordered Ghazni destroyed, leaving behind vast expanses of rubble, barren fields that had once been cultivated, and sand-filled irrigation canals and wells upon his departure from the region in 1223. Some of this devastation left permanent scars.

While Buddhism was almost totally dislodged from the region, Islam gradually gained a much stronger foothold and continued to flourish.

Genghis Khan, the founder of the great Mongol Empire, died in 1227. Following his death, power struggles among ambitious chiefs and princes erupted and intensified until Tamerlane's reign in the late 14th century.

Known for his intelligence and appreciation for art, Tamerlane was a mighty ruler who, apart from Alexander, had conquered much more than any known leader in his lifetime. During Tamerlane's rule, Herat became the Timurid empire's epicenter of art and learning renowned throughout the Muslim world.

By the middle of the 14th century, Mongol rule had lost much of its imperial hold, and the only traces left were the few colonies, such as the Hazaras, that the Mongols had established. Both Marco Polo and Ibn Battutah passed through this region during this era and left records of their observations.

Between 1332 and 1370 this region was ruled independently by the Kurds of Herat until the arrival of Tamerlane, a descendant of Genghis Khan. On his route to India, Tamerlane passed over the Hindu Kush, laying to waste everything in his path; this destruction is evident to this day in the dry waste of the Helmand Valley. Tamerlane was, however, a patron of the arts, and he also organized administration of his lands, constructed public works, and encouraged commerce and industry, introducing new trade routes. Tamerlane's Timurid dynasty lasted about 100 years, during which Afghanistan enjoyed much growth and prosperity.

When Tamerlane's empire shrank, several local chieftains took over different parts of the region. One of them, Buhlul Lodi, captured the throne at Delhi and founded the Lodi dynasty, which lasted for just 75 years. His power, however, encouraged many Afghans to move to India, where they were eventually integrated into the local population.

Babur ("tiger" in Turkish), a Timurid prince and another descendant of Genghis Khan, set out with a few followers on a journey that ended in the founding of the great Mogul Empire of India at the beginning of the 16th century. Babur had a very special affection for Kabul; finding its scenery and climate delightful, he made the city his capital until 1526, when he moved to Delhi. Delhi's strategic and economic importance made it easier for him to administer his huge empire from there. After making Delhi his capital, he never returned to Kabul during the remainder of his lifetime. Still, he asked to be buried in Kabul.

The Mogul armies depended heavily on recruitment among the Afghans of the Sulaiman Mountains. Eventually these ethnic groups played a major role in the disintegration of the Mogul Empire, masterfully pitting the Persians and the Moguls against each other in their struggle to control the strategic areas of the mountain crossroads.

BIRTH OF THE AFGHAN STATE

For a while, the Ghilzai Pushtuns (variant spelling: Pashtuns), under the leadership of a general called Mir Wais Khan, overthrew the Persians and took control of a large part of the Persian Empire. However, because of internal disputes and strife, they lost not only Persia but also Kandahar to Nadir Shah, a Turkish warrior from Khorasan. After defeating the Pushtuns near Jalalabad, Nadir Shah marched through the Khyber Pass to Delhi.

Ahmad Khan Abdali, a member of the Sadozai group and son of a Pushtun chief of the Abdali tribe, was a general in Nadir Shah's army. In 1747, in the skirmishes on the night that Nadir Shah was assassinated, Ahmad Khan fought his way out of the Persian camp, seized a convoy carrying treasure (including the now famous Koh-i-Noor diamond that Nadir Shah had looted from Delhi), and marched to Kandahar.

The Afghans then announced that they no longer owed allegiance to Persia and declared independence under Ahmad Khan, who took on the title of Ahmad Shah, the king of Afghanistan.

Over the next 26 years Ahmad Shah created a single Afghanistan out of what until then had been a land fragmented into distinctly different regions ruled by diverse foreign powers or local chiefs. He took the title of Durrani, or *Doori Dooraani* (DOO-ri-DOO-RAH-ni), meaning the "Pearl of Pearls."

Ahmad Shah Durrani went on to seize all the territories west of the Indus from Kashmir to the Arabian Sea. In 1761, when he defeated the

Babur was a poet of considerable gifts. His prose memoirs, the Babur-namah, *originally written in Turkic, were later translated into Farsi and then into English in the 20th century.*

Mahrattas in India, his empire had reached its zenith. Within 40 years of his death in 1773, Ahmad Shah's great empire fell apart. Bickering and power struggles among his successors led to the downfall of the ruling family. Although his son Timur Shah had 23 sons, he died without naming an heir, and for a quarter of a century after this, the Durrani princes were entangled in a web of intrigue and conspiracy against one another.

When the princes executed the chieftain of the rival Mohamadzais and blinded his eldest son, the latter group rebelled. The dead chieftain's youngest son, Dost Mohammad Khan, defeated the Durrani ruler near Kabul.

ARRIVAL OF WESTERN POWERS

By this time very little of the Durrani kingdom was left, and when the Sikhs began pressing their claims to Peshawar, Dost Mohammad sought military help from the British. The British in India were moving north at the same time as the Russians were moving south into Central Asia. As only the land in the Hindu Kush remained sandwiched between these Western powers, Afghanistan became a pawn between them. When the British refused to support Afghan claims in the Punjab, Dost Mohammad turned to the czar, or emperor, of Russia for help.

The British invaded Afghanistan, precipitating the First Anglo-Afghan War (1838–42). They captured Kandahar and Ghazni. Dost Mohammad fled, and the British placed Shah Shoja, a puppet monarch, on the throne and garrisoned Kabul. The Afghans rebelled, and the harassed British troops were forced to evacuate Kabul. Although the leaders in Kabul had promised safe passage for the British, this promise carried little weight with the Afghans. The British column was massacred before it could reach Jalalabad, and, according to some reports, only one man survived.

Shah Shoja was assassinated by the Afghans, and Dost Mohammad returned to Afghanistan. Before he died in 1863, he managed to unify Afghanistan. Dost Mohammad was subsequently succeeded by his son Sher Ali.

The Russians, having moved their troops to the Afghan border in 1878, sent an uninvited diplomatic mission to Afghanistan. When the British sent a countermission, the group was stopped by Afghan border guards. The British demanded an apology. Unappeased by Sher Ali's explanation, they invaded Afghanistan in December 1878, leading to the Second Afghan War. Sher Ali fled north, seeking Russian help. He was unsuccessful in his appeal and died at Mazari Shareef.

After Sher Ali's death the British placed his son, Yaqoob Khan, in charge; he agreed to all of the British demands, including the appointment of a British adviser. The fiercely independent and proud Afghans found Yaqoob Khan's submission unacceptable. Resentful toward the foreign presence and pressure, they assassinated the British representatives, resulting in the British army's occupation of Kabul and Kandahar. Yaqoob Khan fled to India thereafter.

The attacks by the Afghans against the British, however, did not cease. In 1880, the British eventually relinquished Afghanistan to Emir Abdur Rahman, a grandson of Dost Mohammad, but continued to manage Afghanistan's foreign affairs. The Durand Line was defined to mark the boundary between British India and Afghanistan. The line cut through the region inhabited by the Pushtuns and has been a source of contention ever since. Abdur Rahman was forced to accept from the British as part of Afghanistan the Wakhan Corridor (the remote region covered by the Pamir range), in order to create a buffer between Russia and British India. Reluctantly, he took on the responsibility of controlling the Kyrgyz outlaws located in the Wakhan.

MOVES TOWARD MODERNIZATION

Abdur Rahman's first task was to unite the country—he tried to reduce the power of the various groups by centralizing power in the government. Besides establishing strong control over these factions, the determined leader implemented a string of reforms to modernize the country. His son, Habibullah Kahn, introduced Western medicine, abolished slavery, and founded colleges based on those in Europe.

During World War I, Afghanistan maintained its neutrality despite pressure from its neighbors. When Habibullah was assassinated, his son Amanullah Khan assumed control. To gain complete independence from Britain, Amanullah launched a surprise attack on British troops in India, starting the Third Afghan War. In the peace treaty signed in Rawalpindi in 1919, Britain agreed not to interfere in Afghanistan's foreign policy and relations.

Amanullah angered the conservative families and the mullahs, or Muslim clerics, by introducing drastic reforms to modernize Afghanistan. He abolished the purdah, or the mandatory face-concealing veil for women, opened coeducational schools, introduced Western dress, and started a program to educate the nomads.

The bitter resentment against modernization grew, and in 1928 the Afghans revolted, leading to Amanullah's abdication the following year. After nine months of chaos, Mohammad Nadir Khan, the great-grandson of one of Dost Mohammad's brothers, emerged. An assembly of chiefs proclaimed him Nadir Shah, the next king of Afghanistan.

Mohammad Nadir Khan, or Nadir Shah, based his administration on orthodox Islamic law and set up the Loya Jirga, or Great Council, with all Afghan groups represented. From it, the National Council was formed. An upper house consisting of intellectuals was also created. Political parties, however, were not allowed to operate. Mohammad Nadir Khan abolished

The ruins of the tomb of Mohammad Nadir Khan, or Nadir Shah, in Kabul. Mohammad Nadir Khan was assassinated in the year 1933.

some of the reforms of Amanullah that had angered the conservative elements, and women were returned to the purdah. When Mohammad Nadir Khan was assassinated in 1933, his son Zahir Shah was proclaimed king. During World War II, the new king managed to maintain the country's neutrality and Afghanistan emerged relatively unscathed from the war. The country also prospered under the reforms of Zahir Shah. In 1953 Mohammad Daud Khan, Zahir Shah's cousin, became prime minister. He secured aid from the Soviet Union and began planning to modernize the country. His term as prime minister ended with his resignation in 1963.

Zahir Shah signed a new democratic constitution into law in 1964, with a fully elected lower house and a partly elected upper house. Political parties were still not allowed to operate. In 1973, when the country was devastated and ravaged by a spate of natural disasters, Daud reappeared and overthrew Zahir Shah in a bloodless coup, or a coup d'état. Afghanistan was subsequently declared a republic with Daud as prime minister.

In 1978 Daud was killed in a coup after attempting to crack down on his political foes. This came to be known as the Saur Revolution.

Leaders of the Communist People's Democratic Party of Afghanistan (PDPA) subsequently assumed control of the country. Nur Mohammad Taraki became the president of the Revolutionary Council and the prime minister of Afghanistan. Babrak Karmal was chosen to be Afghanistan's deputy prime minister.

The PDPA was divided into two factions: the Khalq, led by Hafizullah Amin and Taraki, and the Parcham, led by Karmal. Old ideological and ethnic conflicts between the factions soon resurfaced. Thousands of people were killed or imprisoned without trial, and sweeping land reforms and radical social changes were decreed. The black, red, and green Islamic flag was replaced by a red Communist one.

SOVIET INVASION

Armed resistance to the Communist regime, which soon developed into guerrilla warfare, mounted during the winter of 1978. Desertion by Afghan soldiers grew as Soviet advisers tightened their hold over the army, and a network of guerrilla training camps was developed in Pakistan and Iran.

In October 1979 Hafizullah Amin had Taraki killed when it became clear that Taraki, with Soviet backing, was plotting to eliminate him. President Amin's own days, however, were numbered. On Christmas Eve 1979, Soviet troops began landing at the Kabul airport, launching an invasion of Afghanistan. Afghan troops were no match for the well-armed Soviets. Amin was killed after the Presidential Palace in Kabul came under siege, and Babrak Karmal was installed as president by the Soviet Union.

The Muslim groups united into the *mujahidin* (mu-JAA-hi-deen) resistance movement and waged a fierce guerrilla war financed by Pakistan and the United States. Despite their vastly superior arms and resources, the Soviets were unable to defeat the mountain-based rebels. In 1986 Karmal was replaced by Najibullah.

When Mikhail Gorbachev came to power in the Soviet Union in 1985, he began moves to end his country's intervention in Afghanistan. The war was unpopular with the Soviet public and its costs placed a heavy burden on the Soviet economy. It was also damaging to the Soviet Union's relations with other Muslim countries and detrimental to its political interests.

In April 1988 a cease-fire was declared after Afghanistan, Pakistan, the Soviet Union, and the United States concluded a series of agreements in Geneva for a Soviet troop withdrawal. The withdrawal began in May 1988 and was completed in February 1989, leaving the cities in the hands of a pro-Moscow government and the countryside in the hands of the *mujahidin*. Both the Soviet Union and the United States, however, continued to send weapons into Afghanistan. The *mujahidin* were soon armed with increasingly sophisticated weapons.

The Communist regime of Najibullah survived another three years before being overthrown by the *mujahidin* in April 1992. Najibullah, unable to flee Kabul, took refuge at the United Nations compound. Rival *mujahidin* leaders and their parties continued struggling for supremacy.

By the year 1988 there were some 115,000 Soviet troops stationed in Afghanistan. Many countries, including the United States, boycotted the 1980 Summer Olympic Games in Moscow in protest against the Soviet invasion.

CIVIL WAR

General Abdul Rashid Dostum, a Uzbek militia leader, defected to the *mujahidin* units of Ahmaad Shah Masood, a Tajik. In April 1992 fighting erupted between them, the Hizbi Islami under the command of Gulbuddin Hekmatyar, and the Hizbi Wahdat of the Shi'a Hazaras. The Islamic state of Afghanistan was established, but the fighting continued.

THE TALIBAN

Osama bin Laden is the suspected mastermind of the terrorist attacks in 2001. The subsequent hunt for Osama led to the collapse of the Taliban regime and the opening of a new chapter in Afghan experience.

In 1994 a small band of former *mujahidin*, led by a minor commander, Mullah Muhammad Omar, rose up and overthrew the warlord in Kandahar and took control of the province. The Afghan people were weary of the constant fighting among the many *mujahidin* factions, and supported the Taliban. Many from the various ranks and files of the *mujahidin* joined them when they started to occupy the rest of the country.

The Pakistani military also encouraged thousands of Afghan and Pakistani students from the religious schools, or madrassas, and refugee camps throughout Pakistan across the border to join Mullah Omar's partisans. These new recruits were called Taliban, or religious students; hence the name of this movement.

By September 1996 they occupied Kabul, and by 1998, were in control of 90 percent of the country. The remaining opposition was confined to the northeast and the Panjshir Valley. The warlords there formed the Northern Alliance, a coalition of various Afghan factions fighting the Taliban.

The Taliban established a regime of severe religious extremism and were ruthless in imposing their laws. The laws governing women were extremely stringent. Punishment was cruel and swift. Disobedience could mean the death penalty. Religious minorities, such as the Shi'a Hazaras, were subjected to severe atrocities. Many were slaughtered.

The al-Qaeda, an international terrorist network that was an ally of the Taliban and had its headquarters and training centers in Afghanistan, was held responsible for the August 1998 bombings of the United States embassies in Nairobi, Kenya, and in Dar-es-Salaam, Tanzania. The United States, in retaliation, launched a missile attack on al-Qaeda terrorist training camps located in southeastern Afghanistan.

A NEW BEGINNING AFTER THE TALIBAN

Osama bin Laden was suspected of masterminding the attacks on the Twin Towers of the World Trade Center in New York and the Pentagon in Washington, D.C., which occured on September 11, 2001.

The Taliban, however, refused to hand Osama over to the United States. In October that same year the United States, together with the antiterrorist coalition, launched a military campaign targeting key terrorist facilities and political and financial centers. The Taliban disintegrated, and on November 13, 2001, lost control of Kabul.

The anti-Taliban factions, sponsored by the United Nations, met in Bonn, Germany. The Bonn Agreement paved the way for the development of a new Afghanistan. An interim government called the Transitional Islamic State of Afghanistan was set up on December 7, 2001, and Hamid Karzai, a Pushtun leader, was appointed by the UN-led coalition to head this government. Afghanistan, with the help of the international community, thus began its move toward establishing peace, democracy, and political and economic stability. It has since embarked on ambitious efforts in national reconstruction and change.

Crowds of Afghans showing their support for Hamid Karzai in a rally in 2004. The interim leader of post-Taliban Afghanistan was later elected president that same year. After decades of conflict, utter oppression, and bloodshed, a common yearning and desire for peace and national transformation and progress can be felt in the heartbeat of the war-weary nation.

Under the Taliban regime, many were sentenced to death for deviating from the harsh rules of the Taliban.

GOVERNMENT

THE GOVERNMENT OF AFGHANISTAN has undergone several radical changes in the last two decades of the 20th century and first few years of the new millennium. In 1973 the constitutional monarchy of Zahir Shah was overthrown by Daud Khan and Afghanistan was declared a republic.

Daud's efforts to bring about social, political, and economic stability failed. Communism took a foothold in 1978 after Daud was killed in a coup and the Communist PDPA triumphed. In 1992 Najibullah's Soviet-backed regime collapsed, and the Islamic state of Afghanistan was proclaimed.

On New Year's Day in 1994 hostilities again broke out in Kabul and the northern provinces as rival *mujahidin* groups jostled for power in the country. The power struggle among the *mujahidin* factions intensified.

Opposite: **Afghanistan is at a turning point in its violent history. While the country struggles to establish a stable and effective democratic government and a progressive economy, efforts are made to broaden the government's representation of its various ethnic identities. Tribal and group loyalties are still tightly embraced.**

Below: **President Hamid Karzai leads the country's pursuit of change and stability.**

In late 1996 the Taliban, a powerful fundamentalist Islamist militia, gained control over most of Afghanistan despite the opposing forces of the Northern Alliance—a coalition of the Uzbeks, Tajiks, and Hazaras of northern Afghanistan.

The Taliban regime was harsh and oppressive, and it played host to certain Muslim extremists. It remained largely unrecognized in the international community, and its terrorist links led to the implementation of strict economic sanctions against the repressed country by the United States and its Western counterparts.

After the September 11, 2001, terrorist attacks, the Taliban were dealt a devastating blow in a retaliatory attack from the United States and its antiterrorist partners. In early December that same year, Hamid Karzai assumed chairmanship of an interim government put in place after the Bonn Agreement was reached by members of the international community who were committed to help Afghanistan on its path toward democracy and national transformation.

At the Loya Jirga or Great Council held in mid-June of 2002, a constitution was drawn up. This was ratified at the Constitutional Loya Jirga on January 4, 2004.

More than 8 million Afghans, eager to rebuild their nation after decades of conflict and deprivation, voted in the presidential election held on October 9, 2004. Hamid Karzai won a 55.4 percent majority of the votes and was inaugurated as president of the Islamic State of Afghanistan, ending the transitional government.

The country's landmark parliamentary elections for the Wolesi Jirga, or House of the People, and the local councils were conducted on September 18, 2005. On November 12, 2005, after much local and international speculation and anticipation, results of the parliamentary polls were finalized. The winning candidates, or new parliamentarians, belong to and are representative of the various factions of Afghan national life. There is an optimistic sentiment that the country's new democratic inclination will help in the establishment of a common national identity and the pursuit of peace and change.

The Ministry of Foreign Affairs building in Kabul. Afghanistan is a member of the United Nations, and during the Taliban regime there were few diplomatic missions in Kabul, owing to the continuing unrest in the capital. Present-day Afghanistan is receptive to international involvement in its political and economic transition and national reconstruction after the oppressive Taliban. The start of the 21st century marks a milestone in Afghanistan's war-torn history.

THE PRESIDENT

According to the constitution of 2004, the president is elected by popular vote to a term of five years. He must be over 40 years of age, a Muslim, and a citizen.

The president is the head of state and government, and commander in chief of the armed forces. He appoints members of his cabinet, military and police personnel, and provincial governors. These appointments have to be approved by the parliament. His tenure is limited to two terms only. There are two vice presidents. The 2004 presidential election resulted in the victory of President Hamid Karzai.

THE LEGISLATIVE BODY

The Meli Shura (National Assembly) is the two-chambered parliament that is made up of the lower house, Wolesi Jirga, or House of the People, and the upper house, Meshrano Jirga, or House of the Elders.

The Afghan army collapsed in 1992 and disintegrated into factional groups after President Najibullah was ousted. At the time, its equipment included about 1,200 battle tanks.

HAMID KARZAI

Hamid Karzai was born in Kandahar, the fifth of eight children. He is an ethnic Pushtun of the Populzai group, from which many of Afghanistan's kings descended. His father was the speaker of the parliament in the 1970s. The family migrated to Quetta in Pakistan in 1979 when the country was occupied by the Soviets.

Hamid Karzai did a postgraduate course in political science at the Himachal University in Simla in northwest India. He speaks six languages—Pushtu, Dari, Urdu, English, French, and Hindi. He served as a deputy foreign minister in Burhanudin Rabbani's cabinet from 1992 to 1994. He initially considered supporting the Taliban when they rose up, but eventually joined those in opposition to them. Hamid Karzai married a medical doctor, Zinat Karzai, in 1998. On July 14, 1999, the Taliban assassinated his father as he was returning from the mosque in Quetta.

THE WOLESI JIRGA

The Wolesi Jirga consists of 249 members who are elected for a term of five years. Each province is represented in proportion to its population, similar to the U.S. House of Representatives. The number of seats for women must be at least twice the number of provinces.

THE MESHRANO JIRGA

The Meshrano Jirga consists of 102 members. One-third of the members are elected by the provincial councils, and they serve for four years. Another third are elected by district councils of each province and serve for three years. Of the last third, appointed by the president, half must be women, with at least two from the nomadic Kuchis, and two representatives of the disabled. These will serve for five years.

An Afghan woman gets to exercise her right to vote. Her participation is symbollic of the emancipation of Afghan women after the defeat of the Taliban.

The police headquarters in Kandahar. A guard post outside the building was blown up in a suicide bombing in February 2006. Following the collapse of Najibullah's government, the police security forces, together with all the military bodies of the former Communist regime, were combined with the *mujahidin* forces to form a new national Islamic military force.

THE JUDICIAL SYSTEM

The judicial system consists of the Starai Mahkama, or the Supreme Court, Appeals Courts, and lower district courts. The Starai Mahkama has nine judges appointed by the president and confirmed by the parliament for a term of 10 years. The judges are above 40 years of age and are not to be affiliated with any political party. They should hold a degree in law or Islamic jurisprudence. The Starai Mahkama has the power to judge and assess the constitutionality of all laws in the country.

According to the constitution, no law should be contrary to Islamic principles. The state is to create a prosperous and progressive society, based on social justice and the protection of human rights and dignity. It is to be democratic and promote unity and equality among the various ethnic groups. The state should abide by the United Nations Charter, commit to all international treaties and conventions signed by the country, and observe the guidelines in the Universal Declaration of Human Rights.

CURRENT NATIONAL ANTHEM OF AFGHANISTAN

The current national anthem of Afghanistan, *Soroud-e-Melli* was adopted in 2002 and is still used in official ceremonies until a proposed new anthem is accepted.

SOROUD-E-MELLI
(Lyrics as translated from Dari)

Fortress of Islam, heart of Asia,
Forever free, soil of the Aryans,
Birthplace of great heroes
Fellow traveler of the warriors of the men of God,
God is great! God is great! God is great!

Arrow of His faith to the arena of Jihad,
Removing the shackles of suppression,
The nation of freedom, Afghanistan,
Breaks the chains of the oppressed in the world.
God is great! God is great! God is great!

Let the lines of the Koran be our order,
Let the banner of faith be on our roof,
With the echoes and the voices going together,
Let national unity be what we strive for,
God is great! God is great! God is great!

Live happy, live free, live and prosper,
Oh homeland in the light of God's law,
Lift the torch of freedom high,
Become a leader for the people who are oppressed,
God is great! God is great! God is great!

After the collapse of the Taliban regime, the internal security of the country was found to be in shambles. The military and police lacked professional training, guidelines, and rules by which to maintain law and order. They served different factions and were corrupt. The Afghan National Army was soon formed and trained with the help of international forces and trainers in a bid to help the newly democratized country fend for itself eventually.

LOYA JIRGA

The Loya Jirga, or Great Council, is convened only on occasions to decide on matters concerning the country's independence, national sovereignty, and territorial integrity. It amends provisions of the constitution and has the power to prosecute the president.

It includes members of the National Assembly and the chairpersons of the district and provisional councils.

ECONOMY

LANDLOCKED AND DEVASTATED by decades of political chaos, violence, and war, Afghanistan is highly dependent on foreign assistance in its reconstruction and rebuilding efforts. Much of its population still lacks the basic essentials of life. About 80 percent of the Afghan population still resided in rural and undeveloped areas in 2002, and little has been done since to improve their living conditions. Average life expectancy is 45 years. One out of every six children does not reach its first birthday. About 70 percent of the population survives on $2 per day. It was estimated that 53 percent of Afghanistan's population lived below the poverty line in 2003.

Above: **Farmers winnowing grain. The Afghan economy is primarily based on agriculture.**

Opposite: **An elderly roadside barber waits outside an old and partially destroyed building in Kabul. Against the backdrop of destruction, life goes on for the resilient Afghans who have been subjected to the struggles, tragedies, and oppressions in the country's war-torn and conflict-ravaged past.**

In January 2002 the International Conference on Reconstruction Assistance to Afghanistan was held in Tokyo. Sixty-one countries and 21 international organizations attended, and $4.5 billion was pledged toward development in Afghanistan.

After the fall of the oppressive Taliban regime, the end of four years of severe drought, and the generous outpouring of international assistance of $8.4 billion by 2005, the economy of Afghanistan has improved considerably. Yet despite the progress made in recent years, Afghanistan still remains among the poorest countries of the world.

The country faces the challenges of stabilizing and strengthening its economy and national security, eradicating the opium trade and corruption, and grappling with the unprecedented population pressure in the cities as more displaced Afghans return.

A farmer in Nangarhar. Plowing with oxen has been done for countless centuries in Afghanistan.

AGRICULTURE

Afghanistan's economy is predominantly agricultural, and the sector employs about 80 percent of the workforce. The country's main products are wheat, fruits, nuts, wool, cotton, opium, lamb, and sheepskins. Only 12 percent of its land area is suitable for cultivation. Of that, only 6 percent is at present under cultivation. While harvests were abundant during the good times, the endless conflict, hardships, oppression, and natural devastation of the last two decades of the 20th century—war against the Soviet Union, the subsequent civil war, and a severe drought that lasted four years—have impoverished and laid bare many parts of the country. It is estimated that 10,000 farms were ravaged and the country's limited but vital transportation network was badly damaged. The resultant flight to nearby Iran and Pakistan, as well as increasing migration to urban areas, led to a shortage of labor in the fields and further worsened the fall in agricultural production. Millions of Afghans to this day remain dependent on international food aid.

THE FAILURE OF THE HELMAND VALLEY PROJECT

Afghanistan's most ambitious project in the 1950s was the Helmand River Valley project, which attempted to harness the waters of the Helmand and its tributary, the Arghandab. The government signed an estimated $17 million contract with the Morrison-Knudsen Company of Idaho to engineer the project, with the aim to transform hectares of barren desert into an extensive agricultural zone.

Warnings of salinity (salt content), waterlogging, and the thinness of the soil were, however, ignored. Another major drawback was the ignorance of the rural people and their opposition to modernization. The Helmand project became a white elephant that eventually cost the Afghans $55 million and another $60 million in loans and grants from the United States. However, the combined Helmand-Arghandab Valley Authority (HAVA) did bring rural electrification to many of the southern provinces of Afghanistan and did increase substantially the total area irrigated.

At the end of the Soviet occupation, opium became a major cash crop. It represents about one-half of the country's gross domestic product (GDP), or national revenue. Easy to cultivate, process and transport, this has become a quick source of income to the impoverished Afghan. Afghanistan has become the largest supplier of opium in the world during the last decade. Processed into heroin, it is exported, especially, to western Europe. The present government, however, is attempting to eliminate opium production.

Wheat is Afghanistan's chief crop. At the end of the drought in 2003, the wheat harvest was at its largest in 25 years. There was an increase of 58 percent from 2002. However, Afghanistan still had to import an estimated 1 million tons of wheat to meet its domestic demand.

Sugar and cotton have also gained much economic importance, providing raw materials to the growing number of mills. Long before cotton mills were built, raw cotton had been an important export for Afghanistan.

Another significant agricultural activity is fruit farming, which is concentrated mainly in the Kabul and Arghandab valleys. Many of the farms there were destroyed, however, during the turbulent years of warfare. In the valleys, orchards yield apples, pears, peaches, quinces, apricots, plums, cherries, pomegranates, and many varieties of grapes and melons. Such nuts as almonds, pistachios, and walnuts also grow well and, together with fresh fruits and vegetables, are important exports. The main markets are India and Pakistan. Coffee is also exported.

Before 1979 Afghanistan was virtually self-supporting in food, but by 1989 an estimated 33 percent of its agricultural land had been destroyed by the war.

Primitive farming methods are still employed. Plowing is often done with oxen and wooden plows; seeds are not scientifically selected; and land is not properly fertilized. Harvesting is performed manually. The grains are then milled by hand or sent to local mills. The farmers barter their produce in return for meager quantities of cloth, sugar, tea, and other basic necessities.

Livestock rearing, mainly by groups of nomads, is the second most important occupation. The wool, skins, and meat of Karakul sheep are important export commodities. Karakul wool is valued all over the world for its superior quality. It is popular in the United States for making superior-grade Persian lamb coats. Other varieties of sheep are also raised. Cattle provide dairy products. Horses, camels, and donkeys are all used for transport and travel. Goats and chickens are valued sources of food.

Nomads such as the Kuchis have roamed the land with their herds for centuries. However, much of their pastureland is now riddled with land mines from the recent warfare.

At one time much of Afghanistan was covered with forests, but these forests have almost all disappeared. Most remaining timber resources are confined to the mountainous regions of Badakhshan, Wakhan, and the areas bordering Pakistan in the east.

FOREIGN TRADE

Afghanistan's main export partners are Pakistan, India, United States, and Germany. Imports come mainly from Turkmenistan, Kenya, South Korea, Pakistan, India, United States, Germany, and Russia.

The country's main exports are opium, fruits and nuts, handwoven carpets, pelts and hides, cotton and wool, and semiprecious and precious gemstones. It imports capital goods, food, textiles, and petroleum products.

Opposite: **A carpet seller displays his wares. Carpets are an important source of income for Afghans. In 1991 about $44 million worth of carpets was exported to other countries. The international demand for handmade Afghan carpets is still strong and expected to grow given the country's gradually improving infrastructure and expanding trade routes.**

HANDICRAFTS AND INDUSTRY

Afghanistan's industries are agriculture-based. The major industrial crops are cotton, tobacco, madder (used in red dye), castor beans, and sugar beets. The drop in agricultural output has inadvertently affected these industries.

Many Afghans now living in urban areas engage in handicrafts and trade. Every village has traditional small industries, including woodworking, leather crafting, basket weaving, pottery, tile molding, and the hand milling of grains. Metalwork is done in small shops throughout the country, using imported sheets of iron. It is in the towns that agricultural implements, such as plows, spades, pickaxes, and utensils and knives for domestic use are manufactured. Coppersmiths fashion pots, trays, and jugs— those produced in Badakhshan and Kandahar are beautifully patterned with intricate designs.

Afghanistan is also famous for its carpets. The wool and dyes are prepared locally, and the carpets are handwoven. The best carpets can be found in Daulatabad in Faryab Province, near Mazari Shareef, and in Herat. Silk weaving of outstanding texture is made in Herat and the Nangarhar Province. Sheepskin coats of the best quality are made at Ghazni. Silversmiths and goldsmiths all over the country produce jewelry using centuries-old techniques.

45

About 38,500 tons (35,000 metric tons) of salt are mined in Afghanistan every year. Often, sales are made directly at the source to dealers, who furnish the transportation.

Some small industries were started in 1920 by the government. These include tanneries, small machine-repair shops, cotton-ginning mills, bakeries, fruit processing plants, oil refineries, natural gas and coal, as well as soap, shoe, and ceramics factories.

Larger industries include cotton, rayon, and wool mills. Afghanistan also produces its own construction materials and chemical fertilizers.

MINING

Afghanistan has rich, varied, and extensive mineral resources. Its mineral deposits include chrome, copper, lead, zinc, uranium, manganese, asbestos, gold, silver, iron, sulfur, mica, nickel, slate, and salt. Lapis lazuli, amethyst, beryl, ruby, tourmaline, jade, and quartz are just some of the precious and semiprecious gems that have been discovered. Besides these, large deposits of granite, marble, alabaster, gypsum, clay for making china, and soapstone have also been found.

A copper processing plant near Kabul provides 20 percent of the country's needs. The country's huge deposits of iron ore, as well as most other mineral resources, are largely undeveloped because of the lack of adequate infrastructure, including transportation.

Afghanistan is the world's leading producer of lapis lazuli. This deep blue semiprecious gem is obtained from the mines in the Kokcha River valley in Badakhshan and is cut and finished at the lapidarium in Kabul.

Outcrops of coal and seepages of oil and pitch occur both north and south of the Hindu Kush. Promising layers of oil-bearing shale were first found in the north in 1936 by the American Inland Exploration Company. Additional deposits were discovered in the Arghandab River Valley to the west and south of Gardez. In 1954 a Swedish firm began drilling for oil in Jowzjan Province and reported successful finds in 1958. It is believed that Afghanistan has some 242,000 million tons (220,000 million metric tons)

THE ART OF CARPET WEAVING

The art of carpet weaving is highly traditional, and the majority of patterns are jealously guarded family secrets handed down from one generation to the next. The weaving is done mostly by young girls and women, except in Turkoman, where men also weave.

The finest carpets are from Maimanah and are woven from the wool of the Karakul sheep. These carpets have as many as 355 knots to a square inch (55 knots to the square cm), whereas a coarse carpet only has 129 to 194 knots per square inch (20 to 30 knots per square cm). The finest work requires four workers, who take three months to complete a rug of 6.6 square yards (5.5 square m).

Afghanistan has two international airports—at Kabul and Kandahar—through which visitors can enter the country, although the airport in Kandahar is currently utilized primarily for military activities. There are also about 40 local airports serving smaller cities and towns.

of oil reserves. This potential has yet to be exploited, though, not only because of the lack of funds but also because of the seemingly endless wars and unrest.

The most important resource of Afghanistan is natural gas. Natural gas exports made up as much as 42 percent of the country's total exports before the 1990s. Deposits of over 87 billion cubic yards (67 billion cubic m) of natural gas were discovered by the Soviets at Khwaja Gogerdak and Yatim Taq, and production was started in 1967. In the 1980s $300 million a year was earned from the export of natural gas, but most of the revenue went to the Soviet Union to pay for imports and to clear the Soviet debt. In 1989, during the withdrawal of the Soviet troops from the country, the gas fields were capped to prevent sabotage by the *mujahidin*. It is believed that the country has a wealth of about 65.4 billion cubic yards (50 billion cubic m) of natural gas reserves in 2002. Restoration of gas extraction has yet to take place effectively and the country's persistent internal violence and lack of infrastructure, particularly a transportation network and effective government control, have all served to further inhibit efforts to develop or exploit this industry to the country's advantage.

TOURISM

Another source of foreign revenue, tourism, had almost completely disappeared in the last two decades of the 20th century. In the past Kabul used to be a popular stopover for backpackers. In 1990 a mere 8,000 tourists arrived in Afghanistan, bringing receipts of only about $1 million. Some potential attractions for the foreign visitor included Bamian, with its huge statues of Buddha, which were destroyed by the Taliban despite international protest. Work is underway to attempt to restore these statues. Thousands of painted caves, the Blue Mosque of

POSTEENS

Posteens are lambskin vests and overcoats with the fleece turned inward. They are embroidered, usually in the favorite color combination of blue, black, orange, and yellow.

The best *posteens* are made in Ghazni. Women who live in urban areas and villages near towns embroider these and other articles of clothing, including the skullcaps worn under turbans, vests, and burkas or *chadaris*, garments worn by women outdoors that cover the face and body. Color combinations and designs vary in different parts of the country.

Mazari Shareef, the outstanding lakes of Bandi Amir, and the mountains of the Hindu Kush are also of interest. With its stark natural beauty, its unique flora and fauna, and its many historical sites, Afghanistan has much potential for development in the tourist industry, and stability is of paramount importance to its recovery in this sector too.

HYDROELECTRIC POWER

In spring, melting snow from Afghanistan's mountains swells its numerous rivers and waterfalls to gushing torrents with huge potential for hydroelectric power. In summer, when the flow is reduced to a mere trickle, dams and reservoirs are necessary to harness this power. Hydroelectric plants have been constructed in several provinces, including Kandahar, Kabul, and Parwan.

TRANSPORTATION

Afghanistan used to have 13,675 miles (22,000 km) of roads. The Kabul-Kandahar Highway was built in 1960 to connect these two largest cities of the country. It passed through five core provinces, skirting numerous isolated villages. About 35 percent of the population lived within 30 miles (50 km) of this highway, which used to be Afghanistan's lifeline. It had provided access to health care, markets, education, and places of worship. More than two decades of war destroyed the highway. Restoration of this main road was crucial to any development in the country. It has not only been restored since but there are also plans to extend it to form a "ring" road circling through Herat and Mazari Shareef, and back to Kabul.

River navigation is another important method of transportation. There are about 750 miles (1,200 km) of navigable waterways in Afghanistan; the Amu Dar'ya is perhaps the most important. River ports on the Amu Dar'ya are also linked to Kabul by road.

ENVIRONMENT

AFGHANISTAN HAS A VERY FRAGILE ecosystem. The country's arable land and pastures are limited to the valleys and foothills, and the Hindu Kush has sparse vegetation except for the Sulaiman Range in the southwest. This arid terrain covers two-thirds of the country. Half of the rest of the land is desert.

ENVIRONMENT IN CRISIS

Since there was little industrial activity, industrialization's undesirable effects were few, and so changes to Afghanistan's environment were gradual and unnoticed. During the recent two decades of war, its ecosystem suffered

Opposite: **A view of the base of the Hindu Kush mountain range, showing the dry and often harsh conditions that prevail in Afghanistan.**

Below: **A vast expanse of arid land in the Bamian Valley.**

Afghanistan is located in a tectonically active region and is prone to strong damaging earthquakes. Erosion has resulted in avalanches in the Salang Valley.

rapid and irreversible damage. The drought that lasted for almost four years further compounded this.

The decrease in agriculture led to the large-scale migration of Afghans from the rural areas to the cities. The resultant pressing need for urban expansion and development led to the clearing of forests and other precious vegetation.

Rivers, irrigation canals, and wetlands dried up. Water tables were reduced. Water and soil pollution, salinization (a build-up of salt content in the soil), deforestation, and forced migration and resettlement, all resulted in the spread of environmental disease and increased desertification (when land degrades to barren and unproductive soil). Large tracts of forest and farmland were destroyed or burned to accommodate the bulging population.

Chemical weapons were used during the war with the Soviet Union, and Afghanistan's violent recent past left behind a legacy of 10 million land mines peppering the land. Present-day Afghanistan's environment is in crisis.

DEFORESTATION

Until 2000 B.C. the ranges of Afghanistan were covered by dense cedar forest. Although many varieties of forests can be found here, only 1 to 2 percent of its land is forested today. There has been a 33 percent decrease from 1979.

The sharp fall in agricultural production has led to the abuse of the natural resources of the environment. Timber finds a ready market in neighboring countries, and truckloads of timber are smuggled over the border. Other truckloads of wood are brought into the cities to be used as fuel. With the destruction of power plants and electrical cables, wood remains the only option for fuel, and it is used for cooking and for warmth against the bitter cold of winter.

Forests of wild pistachio used to be found mainly in the northwest in the savanna of Badghis Province. Not only did they provide environmental and climatic stabilization, they also provided thousands of families with a livelihood. Wild pistachio nuts used to be a major export of Afghanistan. Much of this forest, however, has disappeared. Roots have been pulled out and exported for use in herbal medicine, and branches chopped up for fuel. Soil degradation due to rampant deforestation has intensified.

In 1999 crops and mulberry trees in the fertile region of Parwan near Kabul were burned by the Taliban military while the farmers were preparing for harvest. These farms were seen as obstacles to the pursuit of war. Vegetation all along the roads was removed for the same reason.

Residents living on the hills of overcrowded cities like Kabul suffer from the high levels of pollution characteristic of urban areas in Afghanistan. The nation, still directing its resources to rebuilding, has to grapple with appalling sanitary conditions and perpetual traffic congestion brought about by its bulging population and poor infrastructure.

A young Afghan village girl looks into the distance, her bright traditional ethnic clothes juxtaposed against the vast expanse of seemingly barren land on which she lives.

About a hundred families occupied an island in the Amu Dar'ya, displacing hundreds of animals as a result.

In Nangarhar Province, in the east, most of the land along the Kabul-Turkham Highway was turned into wasteland.

The large-scale deforestation has led to severe erosion of fertile soils. The topography of the terrain accelerates such erosion. Deforestation has resulted in widespread flooding and in landslides in the Salang Valley, resulting in the loss of many lives. The washing away of topsoil and humus has created ever more arid conditions, and stunted the growth of crops.

WILDLIFE

Afghanistan's fauna consisted of 123 species of mammals. Many of them were rare and native to the region. The Hindu Kush and Pamir mountains were home to rare mountain leopards, gazelles, markhors (a type of goat), Marco Polo sheep, urial sheep, Asiatic bears, and snow leopards. Many of these, it is feared, are now extinct. Caspian tigers are extinct, and fewer than 100 snow leopards survive. Their pelts fetch a very high price on the black markets of the world, making them highly susceptible to being poached. The skins of other such internationally protected or endangered animals as leopards, tigers, foxes, and jackals can be bought all over the country. Marco Polo sheep and ibex are hunted for food.

Afghanistan has 460 species of birds. Among these are birds of prey such as eagles and falcons, many of which are native to Afghanistan. Trade in these birds has recently become common and may lead to their eventual extinction. The Siberian crane is no longer seen there, among other losses. Birds are often captured and caged.

Dynamite fishing has become common and threatens not only the survival of the numerous species of fish in the mountain streams there but also other animals in the vicinity.

The placid and mesmerizing landscape of Bamian belies the country's turbulent past of bloodshed and strife. Given the rough and rugged terrain, Afghans have had to find ways to adapt and overcome limitations imposed by their natural surroundings. However, excessive military and commercial activities have devastated much of the rich natural biodiversity and mineral endowments hidden beneath the imposing façade of aridity.

The many captivating geographical features that the land of Afghanistan is blessed with offer respite from the ecological crisis the country is facing.

Besides this indiscriminate exploitation of nature, the loss of natural habitat also leads to the disappearance and extinction of the distinctive fauna of this country.

POLLUTION

The pollutants from industrial parks of countries of the Aral sedimentary basin, such as Iran, Turkmenistan, and Uzbekistan, contribute to the poor quality of air in cities. Cross-boundary pollution is a threat to Afghanistan's environment as there are too few industries in Afghanistan, yet, to cause much pollution.

Nonetheless, the use of heavy war machinery and weapons for so long has polluted or contaminated the soil in most areas of the country.

With most of the country's infrastructure destroyed, basic sanitation is almost nonexistent. Open sewers are the norm. The water is often contaminated by sewage and contains harmful bacteria such as *E. coli*.

With the return of the refugees, the populations of the cities have swelled, and the heavy demands this has placed on the very weak infrastructure have made the situation very critical, even hazardous, to the environment. The air quality in most cities has deteriorated sharply.

Solid waste disposal is yet another major problem. Most dumps are sited above cities. As a result, their contents and seepage are washed down by the rain, contaminating water supplies and worsening the already dire sanitation problems in the cities.

International organizations such as the United Nations are urging the country to initiate efforts to reconstruct or restore the environment. It is hoped that with a stable government in place it will be possible to work toward preserving and sustaining the environment. If measures to halt further damage are delayed, there may be no turning back.

Young children living in the rural regions and city outskirts are most susceptible to diseases and premature death brought on by escalating pollution levels.

Smoke from the wood fires used for heating and cooking covers the interiors of homes with soot. In the evenings and early mornings the Kabul sky is blanketed with smoke from these fires.

AFGHANS

AFGHANISTAN'S FIRST CENSUS, conducted in 1979, put the country's population at slightly over 13 million. This figure, however, excluded an estimated 2.5 million nomads.

Because of the turmoil and upheaval since then, reliable statistics have been hard to obtain. To escape the civil war, millions of Afghans fled from their homes to safety in refugee camps in the neighboring countries of Pakistan and Iran.

In 1993, after the collapse of Soviet rule, the population was estimated to be 21.7 million, including some 3 million nomads and more than 6 million refugees living just outside the country's borders. In 2005 the population in Afghanistan stood at about 30 million. This is an unfortunate increase for a country in the midst of economic recovery and national reconstruction and transformation after more than two decades of turmoil and war—a war that took the lives of more than 1 million people—and five years of extreme repression under the Taliban. It is difficult to understand how a country that has gone through three decades of violence and tragedy could experience such an exponential population growth.

Like the people of the United States, Afghans are a potpourri of ethnic and linguistic groups. This is the result of the various peoples that entered Afghanistan and eventually intermarried and blended with the local population, leaving their imprint on both the social makeup and cultural development of the country.

Above: **Many Afghan men wear turbans tied in a way that signifies affiliation with an ethnic group.**

Opposite: **Afghan girls eager to begin the day's lesson at school.**

59

The Pushtuns are renowned throughout the world for their prowess on the battlefield. The most successful wars against the British in the 19th century were conducted by the Pushtuns.

Most of the population consists of the Mediterranean subgroup of the Caucasoid race to which most of the people of the Mediterranean and Middle Eastern countries also belong. The Pushtun, Tajik, Nuristani, and Baluchi are Caucasoid.

Besides the Caucasoid, there are two other main physical types in Afghanistan—the Mongoloid and the Australoid. The Hazara, Turkmen (also known as Turkoman), Uzbek, Kyrgyz, and Aimaq are Mongoloid, and the Brahui are Australoid.

PUSHTUNS

About half the country's population is Pushtun. They have traditionally been the most powerful of all the groups in Afghanistan. They regard themselves as the true Afghans. In India and Pakistan they are known as Pathans. As a group, they are still synonymous with strength and fortitude.

Pushtuns appear to have lived in Afghanistan since the beginning of recorded history. Although their origin is obscure, they are believed to be of Aryan stock. Their language, Pushtu, belongs to the Indo-European group of languages and is related to the Persian Farsi.

These people have passed down through the generations a legend about their origin. In one version of the legend, Qais, who is said to have been descended from King Saul and from one of the lost peoples of Israel, is believed to be the person to whom the Pushtuns owe their ancestry. Qais, according to the Pushtuns, was chosen by the Prophet Muhammad to spread Islam in Afghanistan.

In another version, Afghana, a grandson of Saul, is thought to have led his 40 sons to the hills of Ghor in the western part of Hazarajat, making him the ancestor of the Afghans.

The Pushtuns live in an area extending from the Pamir Mountains, north of Afghanistan, across the Sulaiman Range and the Helmand Valley all the way to Herat and the Iranian border. They began venturing out of this mountainous vastness only in the 11th century, when they joined the armies of Mahmud of Ghazni in his conquest of India. Warfare has since then become an integral part of the Pushtun's life; even today the Pushtuns habitually carry firearms.

There are two main Pushtun groups—the Ghilzais and the Durranis, who are also known as Abdalis. The Ghilzais were once nomads who moved around with their herds of cattle and sheep, looking for seasonal grazing grounds. They finally settled in the area between Kandahar and the Kabul River. The Ghilzais came to prominence in the 17th century when the Abdalis were banished by the Shah of Persia.

The Ghilzais seized control of Kandahar, invaded and conquered Persia, and ruled there for a short period. In 1747 when the Durrani ruler

A Pushtun warrior and his ubiquitous rifle.

Ahmad Shah came into power, the Ghilzais were forced to accept his rule. The Ghilzais have always played a crucial role in the commercial and military sectors of Afghanistan.

Physically, the Pushtuns resemble true Aryan stock. They are typically tall and fair, often with aquiline features and black or brown hair and brown eyes, although hazel or even blue eyes are not uncommon.

TAJIKS

The Tajiks are of Iranian origin and, like the Pushtuns, can be divided into two principal groups. One group of Tajiks, who are Shi'a Muslims, lives mainly in the mountainous regions of Badakhshan and the Wakhan Valley. They are farmers who live in villages that are often extremely poverty stricken.

The other group of Tajiks lives around major towns like Kabul, Bamian, Herat, and in the north. They are urban dwellers and form a large part of the middle class in the larger towns. These Tajiks are Sunni Muslims and are skilled artisans and traders. Many are also farmers, and the *zameendars*, or landowners, among them are accepted as leaders. Although tribal organizations no longer exist for this group, a strong communal feeling lives on among them.

The Tajiks are of Mediterranean stock and are generally tall with light skin and black hair, although red or even blond hair is sometimes seen. In the north the Tajiks have more Mongoloid features.

NURISTANIS

In the past, other Muslims often referred to Nuristanis as Kafirs, or unbelievers in Islam. They were called this because they had belonged to an independent group until King Abdur Rahman conquered them in 1896 and converted them to Islam.

A Nuristani man. Nuristanis live in the few forested regions of Afghanistan and use a great deal of timber in their buildings and furniture. Their wooden houses are often two to three stories high. They thresh grains on the flat roof, keep livestock on the first floor, use the second floor for storage, and live on the top floor. Their living quarters often have elaborately carved, open verandas.

Their origins are a mystery as no artifacts or documents that would indicate their beginnings have ever been discovered. For centuries, they remained isolated, and even today little is known about them. Their language belongs to the Dardic group and is related to the Sanskrit of northern India.

Physically, most Nuristanis resemble Mediterranean stock. They are slight of build, with light brown skin, slender noses, above-average height, and black to sometimes blond hair.

Nuristanis are very conservative, place great emphasis on family ties, and are known and respected for their great physical endurance. Nuristani men traditionally wear goatskin coats over a cotton shirt; short, full cotton trousers; leggings; and soft leather boots.

HAZARAS

The Hazaras live among the mountains and valleys of central Afghanistan. Hazarajat is a bare, dry region, watered by canals carefully constructed to carry as much water as possible from the few springs that are to be found. Crop cultivation is limited because of the poor soil and lack of water.

A Hazara family poses for the camera, the father and elder son in their traditional skull caps. The word "hazar" is the Persian word for "one thousand," which could have referred to a division of soldiers in the Mongol army.

Most of the Hazaras are shepherds who follow seasonal grazing grounds. They are hardworking and frugal, but because of the adverse conditions in the region, they have been unable to prosper. Many of them have chosen to join the army, and others have been forced to seek menial labor in the cities.

Hazaras are of Mongoloid stock and are traditionally believed to be descended from the soldiers of Genghis Khan's army that swept through Afghanistan in the 13th century. Most of them are Shi'a Muslims, unlike the majority of Afghanistan's population, who are Sunni.

Hazara men wear skullcaps and are clean-shaven. The women wear long dresses instead of the baggy trousers commonly worn elsewhere in Afghanistan.

64

UZBEKS AND OTHER TURKISH MINORITIES

North of the Hindu Kush area are inhabitants descended from Central Asian Turks, or Tartars. The largest group is the Uzbeks. They are mostly farmers and breed animals, including horses and Karakul sheep. Uzbeks have Turkish features and are usually fairer than other Afghans.

The Turkmen number about 400,000 and live along the southern bank of the Amu Dar'ya. The Kyrgyz, who number about 35,000, made their homes in the narrow Wakhan Corridor. Both groups are nomads of Mongoloid descent.

Another Turkish group, the Qizil Bash, or redheads, so-named because they wore red skullcaps, were taken into Afghanistan by the Persian ruler Nadir Shah in the 18th century to garrison Kabul. Today their descendants, who are Shi'a, occupy a separate quarter of Kabul and Kandahar and are employed in the government civil service and as craftspeople and clerks. Many are also traders.

A member of the Kyrgyz tribe. Most of the Kyrgyz people are Sunni Muslims. Tribal affiliations and loyalties are deeply entrenched in the Afghan individual. The challenge is to forge a single Afghan national identity.

To the north of Afghanistan are several nomadic groups, such as the Kazakhs, Karlug, and Chagatai Turks. These people speak an archaic form of Turkish and often also speak Farsi. The men wear large, soft leather boots, belted cloaks, and turbans. Clothing typical of the area is the greatcoat with sleeves large enough to envelop the hands and to keep them warm during cold weather.

NOMADS

A nomad woman wears an ornamental nose ring and a headband.

As much of Afghanistan's land is barren and arid, it is not surprising that a portion of the country's population is nomadic or seminomadic. The nomads roam the land, moving with the seasons, looking for grazing sites for their herds.

They are fiercely conservative and abhor change. To survive the harsh environment, nomads need to be extremely hardy and tenacious, both physically and mentally. They are proud of their way of life and disdain people who live in cities. The worst thing a nomadic mother can say to a disobedient daughter is, "May you marry a town dweller!"

The Powindahs, also known as Kuchis, are the most well known of the nomads. They are Ghilzai Pushtuns who used to migrate annually across the border into Pakistan in the tens of thousands to trade, their camels and donkeys laden with everything they owned or needed, from their tents to their babies.

Once across the border they sold their wares, such as wool and hides. On their return trip they brought back goods either for their own use or for selling in Afghanistan. The Powindahs traveled at night and camped during the day. This cycle of migration went on for centuries until stopped by a border dispute with Pakistan in 1961.

Powindah men are tall, with piercing eyes and full mustaches. They wear large turbans and are invariably armed with a dagger and rifle each.

The women wear colorful long-sleeved dresses over trousers and cover their heads with long shawls. They also often don heavy silver bracelets on their wrists and ankles and display other ornaments.

These accessories make them look very similar to the Gypsies who roam the length and breadth of Europe and Asia. Perhaps the women's bright clothes and ornaments compensate for the dull, colorless landscape in which they live.

The extreme and discriminatory rule of the former Taliban government, however, decreed that a woman be covered with the burka while outside her home.

OTHERS

There are many groups of Afghans who call themselves *sayyid* (suh-YEED) and claim Arab descent. They speak a form of Arabic.

Thousands of Hindus and Sikhs from the Indian subcontinent have also settled in Afghanistan and can be found mainly in the towns. Most have become Afghan citizens.

The Brahui, who are found in the southwest, are, like the people of southern India, Dravidians, and little is known about how they arrived in Afghanistan and in Pakistan. In Afghanistan, many work as tenant farmers for Baluchi landlords.

INTER-ETHNICITIES

Except for some of the Pushtun areas in the south and the east of the country, few Afghans are of a single ethnic descent. Over the centuries there has been much intermarriage among the different groups in contact with each other in the same regions.

In the north, among the Tajiks and the Uzbeks, a surprising mixture of Caucasoid and Mongoloid features is often found. Red or blond hair and blue eyes are sometimes seen with the epicanthic fold and high cheekbones. Similarly, blue- or green-eyed Baluchis and Brahui, who are normally dark-skinned, are not uncommon.

LIFESTYLE

THE UNWRITTEN LAWS and codes of conduct of *Pushtoonwali* (PUHSH-toon-WAH-lee) reign supreme in Afghanistan. Although basically belonging to the Pushtuns, *Pushtoonwali* is recognized and upheld by all Afghans.

Self-pride and tribe and family honor take precedence over everything else. Life is taken or sacrificed at the slightest hint of insult or loss of honor. Injustices to self or family or even tribe are not easily forgotten or forgiven. Thus feuds can sometimes go on for generations.

Afghan society is patriarchal. The son takes his bride to the ancestral home, where often several generations live together in one home or nearby in the same village. Even when Afghans migrate to towns and cities or move to other villages, family members still get together for important events, and an avid interest is taken in everyone else's affairs.

Every family is headed by a patriarch, and families belonging to a particular ethnic group are, in turn, led by a khan. All important judgments and decisions are made by the local council, or *jirga* (jorhr-GAH). Everyone has a right to voice an opinion, but the final decision is made by the *jirga* and must be adhered to without exception.

Apart from the decision making and the passing of judgment, the khan is also responsible for the safety and prosperity of his village. He must be a person with moral strength, wisdom, piety, bravery, and remarkable hospitality. He must also be of impeccable ancestry.

Above: **A village local council in session. Minor disputes, such as theft and trespass, may be dealt with during these meetings.**

Opposite: **A young Afghan boy sells accessories in one of the many bazaars that dot the arid landscape of Afghanistan. Earning a livelihood for one's family at a young age is common in a country still picking up the pieces after being crippled by decades of war and hardships. Today the cities' education and employment opportunities have to keep up with the burgeoning urban youth population.**

69

The *Pushtoonwali* covers a large area of human behavior, the most important being honor, vengeance, and hospitality. Every child is indoctrinated into its principles from birth. Any breach can be severely punishable, with anything from ostracism and exile to death.

To the Afghan nothing is as despicable as cowardice. Personal or family honor, *ghairat* (gheh-RAHT), must be upheld at all costs. Promises made, no matter what the circumstances, must always be kept.

Fierce family and ethnic group or tribe affiliation leads to the Afghan belief in the right to raid other groups to obtain food and provisions for their own. This is a harsh country, and the availability of water is vital; groups have to compete for what little is available. Life is devoid of all but the most basic material necessities, so a sense of pride and belonging is what makes life worth living. The Afghan is a fighter, battling against the hard conditions of his or her lot in life.

Much of this way of life is left behind when the villager moves to the towns and cities. Society there is no longer classless; the educated and the rich form the upper crust of society. The professionals, teachers, and government and industrial employees make up the bulk of a growing

THE CODES OF *PUSHTOONWALI*
- To avenge blood; to avenge any insult made against one's tribe, one's family, and oneself; to fight to the death for anyone who has taken refuge with one; to defend to the last any property entrusted to one.
- To be hospitable and to safeguard the person and property of a guest.
- One shall not kill a woman, a Hindu, a minstrel, or a boy not as yet circumcised.
- To pardon any wrong, with the exception of murder, at the intercession of a woman, the wrongdoer's family member, a saiyid, or a mullah.
- To punish adultery with death.
- To spare anyone who takes sanctuary in a mosque or shrine. Also to spare in battle anyone who begs for mercy.

middle class. Back home in the villages the elders are revered, and their advice is sought and always heeded. In urban Afghanistan such values no longer hold, and the elderly often feel unwanted and lost.

LIFE IN THE VILLAGES

The villages in Afghanistan are clustered around the larger towns and cities. The flat-roofed houses are built with bricks and plastered with a mixture of mud and straw. In the west, along the border with Iran, and in the northern plains, are found square, domed roofs. In the south the nomads and seminomads build semicircular, beehive-shaped reed huts.

Most houses have enclosed compounds that shelter livestock and boast sheds for storage. In each of these houses, the cooking area and the general living space where the family works and plays also share that compound.

Women walk to the nearest stream or pool to collect water, bathe, and do the laundry. Some of the more affluent households have their own

Arab geographers first wrote about the windmills of Herat in the seventh century. The entire region of what was known in ancient times as Khorasan, along the border with Iran, was covered with windmills, and ruins of windmills were also found in the south, stretching from Kabul and Ghazni to the Indus River. Some historians believe the windmills in Europe and China were inspired by them.

artificially made pools or streams, called *jooyi* (joo-YEE). The trips to the streams provide the women with a chance to get away from home for a while and to socialize with each other.

Accommodation in the villages is always provided for travelers. Where circumstances permit, carpeted rooms are kept to entertain guests in the home. Mosques double up as schools and often also provide meeting places for the local *jirga*. In some villages communal affairs are conducted under shady trees.

Household furnishings are simple, consisting of cooking utensils, basic dishes, and some heirlooms, such as religious mementoes, weapons, brass or copper utensils, and storage chests and containers. Large earthenware pots are used to store grains. Some villagers possess string beds, but most sleep on mattresses that are laid out on the floor at night and neatly stacked in a corner during the day.

The flat roofs are used in summer for sleeping and for drying fruits and vegetables. An earthen platform is often built in front of the house for the same purpose. In summer food is cooked outdoors. Charcoal and dung patties, together with roots and branches, are burned for fuel. The patties are made by the women and children, who collect the manure, form it into patties, and slap them onto walls and rocks to dry.

Mud and brick structures that look like block houses, with rectangular holes for air circulation, are built to dry grapes in order to make raisins. Windmills are found in Herat, but they pump water only during the "time of the 120 days' wind," which falls between June and September.

The Afghans have invented a simple but ingenious system of keeping themselves warm. In the villages south of the Hindu Kush, houses have hot-air tunnels, or *tawkhanah*, built under the floor, and a fire at one end warms up the whole floor. In other places, a small, low table is placed over a charcoal brazier, and a blanket is spread over this table

to contain the heat. The family sits around the table to keep warm. This unique system is called *sandali*.

NOMADIC LIFE

The nomads follow their herds to summer and winter grazing grounds. The seminomads move in summer to pastures with their herds and return in winter to tend crops on their farms. The nomads provide several services to the villagers. Besides supplying animal products, they form lines of communication between different regions. The animal dung left when they pass over the fields helps to fertilize the land. Often the nomads act as moneylenders, lending money to the farmers.

The tents of the nomads are built either with or without frames. Frameless tents are built with black goats' hair. They come in three major styles: the south and western Durrani Pushtun tent; the eastern and northern Ghilzai tent; and the barrel-vaulted tent found in Baluchistan. A fourth style of frameless tent, *arabi*, is found among the Aimaq.

The nomads favor tents that can easily be put up or dismantled. The tents are woven from goats' hair, which is considerably more durable than sheep's wool.

The seminomads live in yurts, tents with a portable latticelike framework. The frame is covered with reeds and a number of woven colored bands. A series of long poles tied with special knots supports the pole at the top of the wood-framed foundation.

The poles are curved to fit into a slotted, hollow wooden disk at the top of the yurt. Felt, often elaborately decorated, is tied onto the frame, with the design on the inside. The door is made of carved wood.

Nomadic migration resembles a military operation. The younger shepherds move along the higher trails with the sheep and goats, while the older people and children move along lower valley trails with the other animals. They may travel 3 to 15 miles (5 to 24 km) a day, and when they stop for the night, the men settle the animals down and stand guard. The rest of the work is done by the women; they put up and dismantle the tents, load and unload the pack animals, do the housework, and prepare the food. Today, much of the land, roamed by these nomads for centuries, is riddled with millions of land mines.

URBAN AFGHANISTAN

Towns in Afghanistan are usually situated at the intersections of major trails or near the larger rivers. Since 1953 asphalt roads have been built in most towns. Towns act as commercial, administrative, and communication centers for the surrounding villages.

Agricultural produce, handicrafts, and raw materials are taken to towns by villagers to be sent on to cities. Transportation within towns is usually by horse cart. Civil servants, who are involved in the administration of the surrounding villages, and landlords, who own land in the villages, generally prefer to live in the towns.

Finished goods from cities are shipped by truck to towns. There, they are sold in the bazaar (marketplace) or the main street of the town; most shop owners live in rooms above their shops. Aside from these goods, various kinds of artisans providing services needed by the villagers can also be found in the bazaars.

Caravanserais (kaarawaansarais), or inns, and *chaikhanas* (chaayikhanahs), or the popular teahouses, are found in the towns. There, the men gather to smoke water pipes, drink strongly brewed tea, and exchange the latest news. The Muslim prohibition against alcohol is almost universally observed.

Unlike in the past, when news was spread solely by word of mouth, there are radios in all *chaayikhanahs* nowadays. News is heard and discussed, and patrons listen to music and songs from Indian movies. Afghanistan has no home-grown movie industry. Indian movies are very popular throughout the country, and there are theaters in all the major towns and cities.

Since antiquity, cities have sprung up where major routes meet and provide access to the outside world. The five main cities of Afghanistan are Kabul, Kandahar, Herat, Mazari Shareef, all with populations of over 100,000, and Kunduz. Kabul is by far the largest city in Afghanistan, with an estimated population of over 3 million.

Just as in the towns, there are bazaars in the cities, on appropriately larger scales. The Kabul bazaar is one of the busiest markets in Central Asia. Almost every kind of merchandise imaginable is sold in its own special section there. Goods produced both on a small scale by individuals and in much greater volume by factories are either sold locally in the bazaars or exported.

Many Afghans migrate from rural areas to the cities in search of employment. This migration increases seasonally when work on the farms ceases. Some stay temporarily and later move back to the countryside, while others settle in the cities permanently.

Shopkeepers in Kabul awaiting customers. Much of the sugar, tea, cigarettes, and soap that Afghans consume are imported from other countries.

Many Hazaras have moved to Kabul. Some become self-employed, trading in wood products, butter, and lard, or making aluminum pots and pans. Most, however, work as laborers, gathering at specific spots every morning for foremen to recruit them. Many Tajiks move to cities to work as drivers. Their hard-earned savings are then mostly used to buy their own land or trucks.

CHANGING LIFESTYLE

After decades of turmoil, the traditional life of both urban and rural societies has disintegrated. At least two generations of children have lost their childhoods. Their minds and bodies are scarred by the death and destruction they have witnessed around them. Dignity and self-reliance were destroyed by living in refugee camps.

With as many as 10,000 villages ravaged and flattened, a large percentage of the rural population has moved to the cities. These, with the millions of returning refugees, have swelled the urban populations.

The government, with aid from such international institutions as the World Bank, has initiated a program of restoration of infrastructures and other public utilities. Clinics, hospitals, commercial institutions, and schools are being built and restored. More than 4 million children have returned to school, and 30 percent of them are girls. Eleven million children have been vaccinated for diseases such as polio and measles.

ROLE OF WOMEN

Women in Afghanistan have traditionally occupied secondary roles in society. They must obey their fathers or husbands and seek their permission for almost everything they do. Nevertheless, women are far from being weak; they wield much power and influence in decision making in their own homes, where they reign supreme as homemakers.

The women of rural Afghanistan are physically strong and work just as hard as the men. They are reputed to be courageous, resilient, and well able to face the dangers of their environment. Most of them have learned to handle firearms and to use them for protection against robbers and wild animals.

In marriage and divorce, Afghanistan follows Islamic laws. A man only needs to repeat "I divorce you" three times in front of a witness to divorce his wife. A woman, on the other hand, has to appear before a judge with reasons for a divorce. Simple though it may sound, divorce is not common. A great deal of social stigma is attached to divorce. Also, the requirement to pay alimony—as well as the difficulty in replacing a wife, who plays an important role in the management of the home, the land, and livestock—makes divorce unattractive to most men. Polygamy is permitted in Islam, and a man is allowed to take up to four wives, a practice that is not very common in Afghanistan. Adultery is punishable by death, according to Islamic laws.

Traditionally, Afghan women followed the practice of purdah. This involves secluding the women from the public eye and confining them to domestic roles and the home. According to the 1979 population census, women made up less than 8 percent of the surveyed work force, numbering just 300,000 out of a total of 3,900,000 workers. Still, they enjoyed greater freedoms than before. The oppressive rule of the Taliban, however, imposed extreme prohibitions on Afghan women, removing what little freedom they had. In March 2005, after the fall of the Taliban, almost half of the government workforce is reportedly female.

Property is usually divided among the sons, the daughters having received their share as dowry. Widows are provided for—a widow receives one-eighth of her husband's property and the assurance of a home and protection by his family. She also controls the jewelry, passing it on to her daughters or daughters-in-law as she likes.

Women in rural Afghanistan enjoy greater freedom than their sisters in the towns in dressing. They do not have to wear the *chadari*, or burka, a voluminous outer garment with only a slit or net for the eyes. The need for them to work side by side with their men in the fields frees them from wearing such cumbersome clothing. However, they must keep their distance from men other than their family members. The women of the nomadic groups move freely, going about their daily affairs unrestricted by rules of gender segregation.

Amanullah Khan, in the 1920s, tried to emancipate women by encouraging coeducation, removing the veil requirement, and promoting the use of Western dress. This angered the religious and conservative elements of Afghan society and contributed to his eventual downfall. During the 1960s and 1970s, under the progressive constitution of Zahir Shah, and during the years of Soviet occupation, many women in the larger cities, especially Kabul, where European influence is most strongly felt, took to wearing Western dress. The Communist government's vigorous effort to improve the status of women constituted one of the reasons for widespread rebellion by conservative Afghans.

Women were denied any freedom or basic rights during the Taliban regime. Purdah and the wearing of the *chadari* had not been enforced in

A *chadari*-clad woman. In the countryside, where the *chadari* is not worn, women cover their faces at the sight of an unknown person.

the past. The Taliban, however, made it absolutely compulsory. Furthermore, a woman was not allowed to leave home without being escorted by a male blood relative. Girls were forbidden to work or to attend school. Now, with the collapse of the Taliban regime, the women in Afghanistan are poised to make new beginnings. Modern dressing has developed and many of their freedoms are restored. Women are liberated from the restrictions imposed on them by the Taliban. Under the new constitution women are on equal footing with men. They are guaranteed 25 percent of the seats in the Wolesi Jirga and 30 percent in the provincial councils. Sixty-eight women have been appointed as new lawmakers after the parliamentary elections of September 2005, marking a watershed in the history of Afghanistan. An Afghan women's rights activist, Malalai Joya, has also been named a new parliamentarian in the Wolesi Jirga.

Many Afghan women have returned to work. There are many female professionals. Nongovernmental organizations, or NGOs, and other groups are conducting classes and lessons for women in crafts such as tailoring. The war has left many Afghan widows to fend for themselves and their children. Others are burdened with looking after men who were maimed or crippled. Postwar Afghanistan seems ready to improve the social position of women and to give women a bigger role in the establishment of democracy in the state. Nevertheless, much still needs to be done to ensure that all Afghan women are given equal career opportunities and that girls are granted a proper education, especially in provinces that still practice strict and sometimes brutal Taliban-influenced gender discrimination.

FAMILY RELATIONSHIPS

Families in Afghanistan are close-knit, and a strong sense of responsibility exists toward all members of the nuclear as well as the extended family. The extended family often includes all those who can trace descent from

In 1985 the face of an Afghan girl was featured on the cover of National Geographic *magazine. Seventeen years after the photograph was taken, the Pushtun girl, now a symbol of the tragic plight of Afghan women and refugees from the war-torn country, was tracked down by the magazine. Her name is Sharmat Gula. The young woman, worn down by years of hardship and toil, now lives in a remote part of Afghanistan with her husband and children. The intense and piercing glare in her captivating green eyes still speaks of the tragedy of a country wracked by a quarter century of war.*

A father and his son in Paktia Province. Families will always take care of their relatives, whatever their own difficulties.

a common ancestor. Similarly, kinship includes those whose ancestors were brothers.

As is the norm in most Islamic societies, there are no family names, and recognition is given by reference to the fathers. In spite of this, the original family of most Afghans is known by all. Any disgrace suffered or honor earned by an individual is felt by all those who claim kinship. Blood relationships are also given due distinction. Paternal uncles are called *kaka* (kaw-kaw) and maternal uncles *mama* (maw-maw). Every kinship tie is well defined and recognized.

Another important aspect of Afghan family relationships is the order of birth. Upon the death of the father, the eldest son, by virtue of his birth rank, assumes authority and becomes the most powerful in the family and receives a larger share of the inheritance.

In urban areas, where Western culture has greater influence, the family unit often consists of the nuclear family alone. When a son marries, he stays with his parents only a short while before moving out to his own home with his bride. The decision to move often depends on the financial position or capacity of the family.

MARRIAGE

In many Afghan stories and folklore, marriage is based on romance. In reality, however, most marriages in Afghanistan are arranged by parents and relatives. There is a strict moral code, and chastity is prescribed for unmarried men and women.

Marriages are often arranged when the couple are still children. But a man does not marry until he is about 18 to 20 years of age or a woman until she is 16 to 18. Marriages between cousins, especially paternal ones, are greatly favored as they are seen to increase or perpetuate the already strong family ties.

In marriages within a family, the bride price, which can often be steep, is forfeited. Otherwise, bride price is paid by the groom's family to compensate for the loss of a valuable family member. A dowry is paid by the family of the bride, and this consists of household goods, which in the urban society include electrical appliances and other modern gadgets.

When the parents decide that their children are ready for marriage, a relative is usually sought to act as go-between. He or she handles the financial negotiations, which may last for months. In some segments of modern society, the services of the go-between are often dispensed with, and the families enter into direct negotiations.

Occasionally, the man and woman are involved in the choice of their own marriage partner, but parental approval is still required. Once the negotiations are complete, several women from the groom's family go to the bride's house for the ceremony of promise. They are served tea and given sweets on a tray that they take home with them. That tray is sent back by the groom's family within the week, filled with money, and then the engagement is announced. Wedding gifts, consisting of jewelry and clothing, are delivered by women from the groom's family before the wedding takes place.

In the country, a wedding lasts for three days, and most of the expenses are borne by the groom's family. The bride's entourage, but not the bride, goes to the groom's home on the first day of the wedding to socialize and to get to know his family. The next day, the groom leads a procession on a horse, with musicians and dancers to announce his arrival.

In the past, if a girl died after the engagement, her family would replace her with another girl from the family. If the husband died after marriage, a brother of the husband would take the widow as his wife. This custom is no longer popular.

Rifles are fired at intervals during the procession. The festivities continue on the third day with a feast, singing, and dancing at the groom's house; various games are played while the guests banter with the groom. In the evening, the procession picks up the bride at her home and winds back to the groom's house; this time the bride rides in the groom's car or in front of the groom on horseback.

The official ceremony, the *nikahnamah* (ni-KAH-naw-MAH) takes place on the third night. The *nikahnamah* is the signing of the marriage contract before witnesses. This ceremony ends with recitations from the Koran by the officiating mullah and the throwing of sugared almonds and walnuts onto the bridegroom.

In the cities, the more Westernized Afghans no longer hold such long and elaborate weddings. They combine all the ceremonies so that the wedding lasts for only a day, with the rituals usually occurring at one of the popular restaurants. Most of the guests and even the groom wear Western dress; the bride is still likely to wear a traditional green or red velvet dress.

CHILDREN

A midwife is always available, even among the nomads, to assist the mother at childbirth. There is a great deal of rejoicing, especially if the baby is a boy. The celebrations may go on for as long as three days, with guns being fired, drums beaten, and food distributed to the poor.

On the third day the baby is named, usually by its paternal uncles. Among the more urbanized families, the parents choose the name. The mullah first whispers "*Allah-u-Akbar*" ("God is great") in the baby's ear and then whispers its name. He also informs the baby about its ancestry and exhorts it to be a good Muslim and to uphold its family's honor.

Among the nomads the oldest paternal uncle gives the child its name and assumes a role similar to that of a godfather in Christian societies. He will be responsible for the child if the father dies.

The birth of a boy has greater significance because he will be an heir. He will be indoctrinated from a young age with the principles of *Pushtoonwali* and expected to uphold the good name and honor of his family. Girls are usually not ill treated, but their needs always come second to those of the males in the family, and they may even be neglected. All children are brought up in the women's quarters. The mother breast-feeds the child until the next baby comes or the child is too old.

Children are toilet-trained by their mothers when still very young and taught to feed themselves. It is the mother who must discipline the children; their fathers usually indulge them. However, it is the father who usually bathes and dresses his little sons.

The women in Afghanistan wield power in family affairs, and the participation of men in some family duties is seen as an example of women's influence. Men who are favored by the women of a household also have greater say in domestic matters.

In rural societies young boys learn to watch over the animals as they graze. Unlike in Western society, there is no marked adolescence. When a boy is about 7 years old, he leaves the women's quarters and is circumcised, usually by an itinerant barber.

A feast is held, with games of physical skill and prizes of money or expensive turban cloth given to the victors by the boy's father. After this, the boy is treated as a man; he is allowed to wear a turban or a cap and is expected to take care of himself. He must begin to help his father in the fields. A nomad child learns to ride and shoot, and watches the herds.

No ceremony marks a girl's arrival at puberty, but in certain areas, especially Paktia, molasses is distributed among the women as a special

In the cities, a baby's birth is celebrated on the seventh day. At this celebration the baby is named. The guests bring gifts for the newborn, and there is singing and dancing in the women's quarters. Based on research conducted by the Afghan Ministry of Health in 2002, the average maternal mortality rate in Afghanistan is a shocking 1,600 in every 100,000 births. About 515,000 Afghan women die in the country every year due to pregnancy and childbirth. One of every six Afghan children does not survive the first year of life.

Although more Afghan children are attending school today, and efforts are made to extend educational opportunities to the rural populations, in February 2005 Afghanistan's National Human Development Report stated that Afghanistan, with its unfortunate lack of teaching facilities and buildings, as well as a shortage of trained teaching professionals, has "the worst educational system" in the world.

treat. The girls help to look after their younger siblings and, like the boys, watch over the grazing herds. By the time they are about 9 or 10, they have learned the skills to be a good wife and mother. They are able to grind wheat and corn, fetch water, cook, sew, clean, and make dung patties for fuel.

EDUCATION

Until the early 1900s the only education available was at mosque schools, which were attended only by boys. Girls acquired their religious training from elderly women, who conducted classes at home.

King Habibullah founded the first modern school in Kabul, in 1903. He refuted opposition from the mullahs with the argument that providing an education was deemed an obligation by the Prophet Muhammad. He patterned the school on the Aligarh University in India and called it Habibia. Secular as well as Islamic subjects were taught. By the time of World War I, foreign teachers had been added to the staff.

King Habibullah also founded a military academy for army officers and a training college for teachers. Education made further rapid strides under the reign of King Habibullah's son and successor, King Amanullah, when a number of schools were opened in urban as well as some rural areas.

Habibia had by then become an academic high school patterned on the French secondary school system, and its first high school class graduated in 1923. Four more high schools were opened in Kabul and other major towns between 1923 and 1928. The first school for girls was opened in Kabul in 1924. The constitution of 1931 made primary education compulsory and free for all children. However, by 1940 there were still only 250 primary schools for boys, and even by 1967 the government had not succeeded in providing adequate facilities.

After World War II, Afghanistan's educational system was greatly influenced by the United States, Britain, France, and Germany. During the 1950s more girls' schools were opened in spite of opposition from conservative Afghans. Progress in education was often slow because of poor attendance. In rural areas parents were reluctant to forgo their children's help in the fields, and many children could not attend school for several months during the winter because they could not get there. Moreover, educating the children of nomads was difficult. Mobile schools and traveling teachers were introduced to address this problem.

Village schools are often run by a single person and modeled on the religious or mosque schools. The different languages spoken even in one area present a major problem. The official language of the school is the first language of the majority in the region. The Koran, however, is taught everywhere in Arabic.

A teacher conducts a class in an open-air village school. Since 1979, higher education has been disrupted by the departure of much of the teaching staff from Afghanistan. In the late 1980s, more than 15,000 young Afghan students were sent to colleges and institutes in the Soviet Union and eastern Europe. With the fall of Communism and the collapse of the Taliban regime, efforts are extensive at improving the quality and availability of education and training opportunities for every section of Afghan society.

By 1967 there were some 58 vocational schools offering courses in agriculture, technology, commerce, economics, arts and crafts, tailoring, secretarial services, and home economics. In addition, there were special training programs in civil aviation, community development, accountancy and finance, radio operation, and nursing.

Higher education began in 1931 with the founding of the College of Medicine at the new Kabul University. This was followed in the 1940s by the faculties of law, science, and literature. In 1946 Kabul University was formally established. Originally, as a concession to the conservative segments of society, separate departments of medicine, science, and letters were run for women. By 1960 all faculties were coeducational.

During the Soviet occupation, of the 1.57 million school-age children in refugee camps, no more than 20 percent received formal education of any kind. Higher and secondary education was even more badly affected, as there were only about 145 high schools for hundreds of thousands of students. With only 78 primary schools for girls, their education was negligible. There remained a great deal of prejudice against educating girls. Most schools in the refugee camps were run by Christian organizations, and their influence was feared by parents.

At present the education system in Afghanistan is in the process of being reconstructed. The destruction of infrastructure and the unstable conditions in the country have led to the exodus of teachers and qualified instructors. Under the Taliban rule, girls were not allowed to attend school at all and many schools were destroyed.

It is now hoped that by 2015 at least 13 million children will be in school. An approximate $3 billion is budgeted on upgrading education. There is a need to train teachers, print textbooks, and rebuild or renovate schools. In 1993, of the 45,000 children in school, only 19 percent were girls. Latest statistics show that of the more than 4 million in school, one-

third are girls. The enrollment of children between 7 and 13 years of age has increased to 54 percent (67 percent for boys and 37 percent for girls). The distance to schools, poor facilities, and the lack of separate schools for girls in areas still steeped in the Taliban doctrinal legacy deter the increase in enrollment.

Higher education can be attained in the country. There are six main universities, including the University of Islamic Studies and two training centers for teachers.

REFUGEES

Afghanistan had the largest refugee repatriation in the world in the last 30 years, though approximately 3.5 million Afghan refugees still remain in foreign countries. Between January and October 2004, 740,000 returned to Afghanistan. Of these, 45 percent came from Pakistan, 53 percent from Iran, and the rest from other countries.

In support of Afghan refugees and other displaced conflict victims, the United States contributed $300 million between September 2001 and March 2005.

Kyrgyz children read their books inside a yurt. The total enrollment at primary and secondary schools, as a proportion of the school-age population, dropped from 29 percent in 1981 to only 19 percent in 1989.

HEALTH CARE

Afghanistan's swelling population makes the availability of proper medical services an absolute and vital need. With help from the international community and the World Health Organization (WHO), the government is rebuilding and improving primary health care. Tuberculosis remains a serious health problem, and 162 facilities for its treatment have been built in 141 districts across the country. The success rate in treatment was 82 percent in 2002. To combat malaria, 600,000 individuals are given full treatment every year. With the assistance of the WHO, mosquito nets have been provided to 750,000 people.

In a serious bid to improve health care and reduce infant and child mortality rates, health-care officials make trips to both urban and rural households to administer immunization against polio and measles.

DEATH

When a Muslim is on his or her deathbed, family and friends gather around to recite verses from the Koran and lament. Often these expressions of sorrow can be very loud and dramatic, even though Islam advocates the acceptance of death as an act of Allah.

Once a man dies, his male relations, with the help of the mullah, who recites prayers, bathe the body. Female relations do this for a deceased woman. The ritual ablution, which is normally done in life before the daily prayers, is performed on the body. The toes are tied together, and the body is then shrouded in white cloth.

The body must be buried as soon as possible, but never at night. In the country it is taken to the mosque, where a prayer for the dead is said. In urban Afghanistan the body remains at home while a prayer service is held at the mosque. Occasionally this service is held at the graveside.

The grave must be about 6 feet (1.8 m) long and at least 2 feet (0.6 m) deep to allow the corpse to sit up on the Day of Judgment. The feet must point toward Mecca so that when the corpse sits up, it will face the holy city of Mecca. In some areas the body is buried on its right side, with the face toward Mecca.

Pottery or stone lamps are lighted on the grave, and for a year, prayers are said for the deceased every Thursday night. On the 14th and 40th days, close relatives and friends visit first the grave, to offer prayers, then the deceased's home, where the family will have prepared a meal. The same ritual is held after a year. On the first anniversary of the death, the women of the family, who have worn only white, the color of mourning, for that period, visit the gravesite to be released from mourning.

Many rituals and beliefs are throwbacks to the practices of pre-Islamic times. Head and foot markers on graves in Nuristan look very much like grave effigies from Kafir, or pre-Islamic, times. In Pushtun areas, a narrow white cloth is tied from the head to the foot of a grave. When this strip breaks it is believed that the soul has escaped to purgatory to await the Day of Judgment. It is also believed that the damned soul of an improperly buried person can return to kill or enslave other souls and can be controlled only by practitioners of black magic. Afghans never remove any plant from a graveyard, for this is believed to bring death to the family or release an evil spirit that may be imprisoned in the roots.

An elaborately carved grave in the province of Nuristan. When an Afghan dies, neighbors often send food and money, and lend emotional support.

RELIGION

TOGETHER WITH CHRISTIANITY, Islam is one of the major religions of the world. Although the Middle East has traditionally been the stronghold of Islam, the religion also has hundreds of millions of adherents throughout the rest of the world, with sizable populations in countries such as Pakistan, India, China, Indonesia, Malaysia, and the United States, where some five million Muslims live. Muslims are what Islam's followers are called.

Islam was founded by the Prophet Muhammad in Mecca in the seventh century. Muhammad, according to tradition, received revelations from God through the angel Gabriel when he was about 40 years old. The word for "God" in Arabic, and as used throughout the Muslim world, is "Allah." These revelations were compiled and written in the Koran and form the basis for the tenets of Islam. Islam shares some Judeo-Christian beliefs, such as the existence of only one God (in this case, Allah), the account of Abraham, and the angel Gabriel.

Afghanistan has been an Islamic state since 1992 when the various *mujahidin* groups succeeded in overthrowing the Soviet-backed President Buhannudin Rabbani. More than 90 percent of the population is Muslim. Most Afghans are Sunni Muslims, and the remainder, mostly Hazara, are Shi'a Muslims. There are doctrinal disagreements between the Sunni and the Shi'a Muslims that influence events to this day.

Nevertheless, Islam forms an extremely strong bond among the diverse peoples of this country. Their strong faith in their religion spurred the Afghans to withstand the Soviet onslaught. The tenets and beliefs of Islam guide its adherents in any given situation, whether personal, social, economic, or political.

Islam not only dictates the religious observances and rituals but also lays down laws for almost all aspects of everyday life. Because of this, the mullahs have held extensive power over much of the Afghan lifestyle for centuries.

In the eighth century all of the Prophet Muhammad's known sayings, decisions, and responses to various life situations, and to philosophical and legal questions, were brought together in the Sunnah (SOON-nah). The Sunnah, commonly known as the "Prophet's traditions," forms the second source of the Islamic faith and law after the Koran.

Opposite: **About 90 percent of Afghans are Muslim. Here in the city of Kabul, Afghan men pray at one of the main mosques.**

The increase in secular education and greater urbanization in the 20th century have eroded some of the mullahs' influence. However, with the *mujahidin* groups now in power, Islam can be expected to take on an even greater role in every Afghan's life.

THE FIVE PILLARS OF ISLAM

Islam imposes five main obligations, or pillars, on its followers. These laws are written down in the Koran, the basic source of Islamic teachings.

SHAHADAT The most important principle of Islam is the belief that God (Allah) is the one and only deity and Muhammad is His prophet or messenger. This, the first pillar of Islam, is called the *Shahadat*. Anyone who converts to Islam must take an oath that on the Day of Judgment he or she will bear witness to this belief.

SALAT This refers to prayers, which form the second pillar. After ritual washings, a Muslim must pray five times a day, facing toward Mecca, Islam's holy city. The prayers must be said at dawn, immediately after noon, in the late afternoon, at dusk, and at night.

The faithful are called to these prayers by the muezzin (moo-EZ-in), using the call to prayer known as the *Azan*. The prayer may be performed alone by the individual or with the congregation in a mosque. Praying in a mosque is more usual for Muslim men than women.

Women who go to the mosque must pray in an area set aside for them. Friday can be considered as the Muslim Sabbath, although they do not call it that. All must gather for the noon prayer at the mosque, and a sermon is delivered by the religious leader of that community or by an Islamic scholar.

ZAKAT Every Muslim must give a certain percentage of his personal wealth to the poor each year. This is usually done in the month of Ramazan (RAM-ah-ZAHN), called Ramadan (RAM-ah-DAHN) in other parts of the Muslim world. This is the month when Muslims fast. The payment, or *zakat*, may be made directly or indirectly, through the clergy or the government. In Afghanistan the traditional amount is two and a half percent of one's annual income. This act is believed to purify a Muslim's possessions.

SAWM During the month of Ramazan, the ninth month of the Muslim calendar, no food or drink may be consumed between dawn and dusk. The act of fasting is called *sawm*. The dawn meal, called *sahari*, is eaten to sustain the individual until dusk, when the fast is broken with the evening meal, known as *iftar* (if-TAAR).

In most towns and villages the times for these meals are announced from the mosque. In Kabul the cannon on Sher Darwaza Hill is fired an hour before sunrise so that people can wake up and eat. The second time the cannon is fired, all eating must cease. At dusk the cannon is again fired to announce the end of the fasting.

HAJJ The hajj is the pilgrimage to Mecca in Saudi Arabia, where the Kaaba, believed by Muslims to be the House of Allah on earth, was built

It is the duty of every Muslim to visit the holy city of Mecca in Saudi Arabia at least once in his or her lifetime, unless prevented from doing so by reason of poverty or illness.

Opposite: **Kyrgyz children learn to read the Koran. As the Koran is in Arabic, learning the language is a prerequisite. Many educated Muslims memorize passages from the Koran, making it a lifelong task. The meanings of passages that refer to rituals and living guidelines have to be interpreted and understood and not simply memorized.**

There are similarities and differences between the Koran and the Bible. The Koran recognizes a line of prophets, including Moses and the prophets of the Old Testament, but Muslims believe Muhammad is the last in the line. Like the Bible, the Koran affirms the existence of angels as God's messengers, but it also mentions jinni, or spiritual beings created from fire. Rebellious jinni are called demons, and Satan is believed to be the chief demon.

by Abraham at Allah's command. On the ninth day of the 12th month of the Islamic calendar, the pilgrim must perform set rituals and prayers at the Kaaba and in other strategic places in its vicinity. The next day animals are slaughtered as a sacrifice to Allah and to commemorate the slaying of a sheep by Abraham, in place of his son, at Allah's command.

SHI'A AND SUNNI

After the death of the Prophet Muhammad in 632, there was disagreement over his successor, and his followers split into two groups. The Sunni, or Sunnite Muslims, believed that his successor should be elected from among the prophet's companions. The Shi'a, or Shi'ite Muslims, believed that the prophet had appointed his son-in-law and cousin, Hazrat Ali, as his successor.

Over the centuries, other differences between the Sunni and Shi'a evolved, but the original dispute over the succession to Prophet Muhammad remains the most crucial of the differences. Today more than 90 percent of the world's estimated 1.3 billion Muslims are Sunni. Afghanistan's neighbors Iran and Iraq have Shi'a majorities.

Most Afghans, about 80 percent of the population, are Sunni. The Shi'a minority is made up of the Hazaras, the Qizil Bash, and many Tajiks. The Ismailee Muslims, whose faith is an offshoot of the Shi'a, are found among the mountain Tajiks. Afghans believe that Hazrat Ali is buried in Mazari Shareef.

PRE-ISLAMIC BELIEFS

The religious beliefs of rural Afghan Muslims are still mixed with the superstitions and rituals of their pre-Islamic past. Most villagers believe in the influence of good and bad spirits and try to placate them. Jinni, mentioned in the Koran as spiritual beings, are thought to threaten women and children with evil. As such, amulets and talismans are acquired and worn for protection against the jinni.

THE JIHAD

Sometimes referred to as the sixth pillar of Islam, the jihad is, in theory, the permanent struggle to make the word of Allah supreme. The Koran advocates using the sword only as a last resort. Disbelievers, according to some passages in the Koran, should be guaranteed the freedom to practice their own religion.

The concept of the jihad has been abused by unscrupulous Muslims throughout history. To the Afghans constantly involved with war, however, the jihad has taken on great meaning.

Throughout the years of the Soviet occupation, the jihad was the main driving force of the Afghan *mujahidin*. Those killed in the confrontation with the Communists were called *shuhada* (shoo-hah-DAH), or martyrs, and are buried in a martyrs' cemetery (*right*).

For some Muslims, the jihad can also be interpreted as a sacred or holy struggle against any enemy—real or abstract, such as poverty and other social illnesses—that may impede the progress of an Islamic society.

There are numerous shrines, or tombs of saintly persons, in Afghanistan. Women, especially, go to these to receive blessings or to ask for special favors. To make a wish or to swear vengeance, a piece of colored cloth is tied to a stick buried near the shrine.

NON-MUSLIMS

Non-Muslims make up a very small portion of Afghanistan's population—just 1 percent. They are predominantly urban dwellers. Despite their small numbers, Sikhs, Hindus, and Jews have played leading roles in the country's commercial life. Many have contributed much to the socioeconomic well-being of the country and brought about much progress in many sectors that had been left untapped and undeveloped due to war and militancy.

A small community of Parsis, who are Zoroastrians originally from Persia, has remained in Afghanistan. But of other older religions that had strong connections with Afghanistan in ancient times, nothing remains.

LANGUAGE

AFGHANISTAN'S MANY ETHNIC GROUPS speak a great variety of languages. The two most important languages are Pushtu (variant spelling: Pashtu), the language of the Pushtuns, the largest group in the country, and Dari, a language similar to Persian. Both Pushtu and Dari are official languages in Afghanistan, and most Afghans will understand at least one or the other in addition to their original tongue.

Many of Afghanistan's languages, including Pushtu and Dari, have a common root in the Indo-European language family. The Pushtuns, Tajiks, Hazaras, Aimaq, Baluchis, and Nuristanis speak Dari or Pushtu. The other major language family in Afghanistan is Turkic, which is spoken by the Uzbeks, Turkomans, Kyrgyzs, and other Turkish groups. Turkic languages predominate in the northern regions.

THE INDO-EUROPEAN LANGUAGES

The Indo-European group of languages includes the languages of Iran, India, and Pakistan, as well as most of Europe. Scholars believe that the Indo-European languages were brought to these sites by Aryan invaders about 3,000 years ago. All the different languages of the Indo-European family have the same structure, and many of the words in their vocabularies sound similar as they stem from the same linguistic matrix.

Most Pushtuns speak Pushtu. The Tajiks and some of the urban Pushtuns speak Dari. The Hazaras use Hazaragi, which is a dialect of Dari. The distribution of dialects and languages forms a pattern related to the different geographical regions. In the southwestern plateau Pushtu predominates. In the northern plains and central highlands Dari, Uzbek, and Turkic are spoken, whereas in the northeastern region Dari and the various languages of the Dardic branch of the Indo-European family enjoy wider usage.

The nomadic way of life of many Afghans makes it necessary for them to speak more than one language. They travel to different regions of the country not only with their herds but also for business.

Opposite: **An Afghan woman reads the newspapers. The *Kabul Times* and *Kabul Weekly* are among the few more widely circulated papers in the cities of Afghanistan.**

Dari is often used for communication between different groups as most Afghans speak Dari. In the 1930s, during the reign of Zahir Shah, the government tried to promote the use of Pushtu. For example, in 1936 Pushtu was declared the national language of Afghanistan. Dari, however, prevailed because of its importance in literature and because it is the language most used by the business community of the country.

Various ancient Indo-European languages are spoken by small communities living in the Pamir Knot region in Badakhshan and in the Pamir Mountains. Among the more important groups are the Sughnis, the Wakhis, the Munjanis, and the Zebakis. Each local variant may have only a few thousand speakers.

SHARED LANGUAGES

Most of the languages spoken in Afghanistan are also used in neighboring countries. Besides Dari, which shares its roots with Farsi, spoken in Iran, Uzbek and Turkic are spoken in the Central Asian republics of the former Soviet Union. Many Pakistanis also speak Pushtu, and Baluchi is common to the Baluchis who live in both Afghanistan and Pakistan. Tajiki is the Persian dialect spoken in Tajikistan and in parts of Uzbekistan. Khorasani, spoken by Persian speakers in the west and to the north of Kabul, is yet another Dari dialect.

The main Dari dialect found in Afghanistan is Kabuli, which is used by the majority of the educated elite. The structure of the Aimaq language is Iranian, but its vocabulary borrows heavily from Turkic languages. Hazaragi, spoken by the Hazaras, is a Dari dialect, too, but also contains many Turkic and Mongol words.

Punjabi and Sindhi are the main Indian languages spoken in Afghanistan by Hindus and Sikhs in the urban centers of eastern Afghanistan. Hindu merchants sometimes use Urdu as a language of trade.

All the different languages are again divided into dialects, each with a different pronunciation and vocabulary. Except in the case of extreme dialectical variation, most people speaking the same language can understand its dialects. Afghans who are not native Dari speakers, for example, usually know enough of the language to communicate with those speaking other languages.

SCRIPT

The many languages found in Afghanistan have a common factor: they are all written in the same Arabic script, from right to left. The Arabic characters are supplemented, as needed, by the addition of diacritical marks to represent sounds that do not exist in Arabic. Because so many languages in Afghanistan are related, anyone who has learned the expanded alphabet can read the script of these languages.

Afghans bargaining at a bustling street market in Afghanistan. Some Pushtu, a little Dari, and perhaps a smattering of Uzbek and Turkic are likely to enter conversations at markets.

FOREIGN LANGUAGES

English, French, German, Italian, and Russian are spoken by some of the educated Afghans as these languages were taught in some schools before the Taliban regime. The literate among the Afghans can often speak not only a couple of other Afghan dialects besides their mother tongue, but also a few non-Afghan languages. It is not uncommon to meet officials who can speak as many as four or five languages, including English and Urdu.

Many Afghans who speak English acquired the language while working. Frequent contact between Afghans and the British in India gave the nomads and those who served in the army the chance to communicate in English. Many others learned English while working for the U.S. company involved in the Helmand Valley project and other U.S. ventures in Afghanistan during the 1950s.

THE PRESS IN AFGHANISTAN

The first newspaper in Afghanistan was published in the middle of the 19th century during the reign of Ameer Sher Ali. The Persian-language *Kabul*, later known as *Shams-un-Nahar*, published the latest happenings at the royal courts and lasted until 1879.

After World War I Amanullah Khan had used the press to popularize his modernization campaign, and during his reign, no fewer than 15 newspapers were in circulation. Freedom of the press was provided by the constitution of 1931 and made more specific by Article 31 of the constitution of 1964. However, a new press law was enforced in 1965 that specified the conditions and limitations governing the publication of newspapers.

Since the overthrow of the Taliban, the media in Afghanistan has started to flourish. Many new publications have been launched, including several for women. In 2002 the *Kabul Weekly* was finally published again after five years of silence. The government needs wide press coverage to get their messages across to a people widely divided not only geographically but also culturally and politically. The new laws on freedom of the press are quite lenient, but starting anything in one of the poorest countries in the world is no easy task. Communications infrastructure is very rudimentary, less than 40 percent of the population is literate, and not many buy newspapers.

Afghanistan had one of the highest levels of adult illiteracy in Asia, with an average rate of 70 percent in 1990, according to estimates by UNESCO. Only 36 percent of the population, however, is literate by 1999, and that did not change by 2005.

BODY LANGUAGE

Afghans use a great deal of body language in expressing themselves. There is also much physical contact among members of the same sex. Any touching between opposite sexes is strictly forbidden, in keeping with Islamic doctrine.

When greeting friends and acquaintances, Afghan men often clasp both hands in a firm handshake and hug and kiss each other on the cheeks to express warmth and camaraderie. Unlike in Western countries, they are not self-conscious walking arm-in-arm with other men.

In business dealings, contracts or agreements are sealed with a firm nodding of the head.

Opposite: **A busy shopping alley in Kabul. The languages used in Afghanistan are mainly Pushtu and Dari (Afghan Persian).**

101

در عهد فرخنده ولی‌عهد دین‌پرورانه اعلی‌حضرت محمد ظاهرشاه پادشاه معظم جلاله‌الله سلطان ماضی‌الدین ظفریت سلطنت در شاه غازی
شهید سعید رحمةالله علیه که صدر درخشان شان در ده نهضت جدید وبختیاری مملکت و احترام و حفاظت و اعمار مزارات متبرکه و آبادات تاریخی وطن مخصوص اطراف
توجهات شاهانه‌شان واقع بوده در حجره بساعه ... امانت زهم عام المنفعه دیگر دین وله ... درستا سر مملکت تعمیر این طاقین و اق فعل نبی رفضیه طهره حضرت شاه ولایت اسماء
اسماء اقطاب قین ایتاب حرام ... جده شید میرزا جانب نصرت جمال الدین علی الرحمه ... بای اطراف و تصه شریف اصلاحات مجدد شهر طراز مغرب سال ۱۳۱۹ شمسی ماشیجام

۱۳۱۹

ARTS

AFGHANISTAN HAS A RICH CULTURAL heritage covering more than 5,000 years. Little new or original art, literature, or architecture, however, has been produced since the 17th century, when rivalry between the Persians and the Moguls began. This is primarily because there have been few prolonged periods of peace in the country since then.

PRE-ISLAMIC HERITAGE

Great archaeological findings include the rock and pillar edicts of Ashoka the Great, which were erected to preach Buddhism and encourage pacifism by his subjects, and the ruins of the ancient Greek city at Ai Khanoum. It was in ancient Afghanistan that the artistic and architectural styles of the Greeks, Buddhists, and the Indus River civilizations fused to yield the Greco-Buddhist and Gandharan schools of art.

A banner that once hung over the entrance of the Kabul Museum reads, "A nation stays alive when its culture stays alive."

Left: **Buddhist frescoes discovered in the caves of Bamian. Buddhism, the religion founded by Gautama Buddha in India in the sixth century B.C., was first introduced in Afghanistan by rulers of the Mauryan Empire.**

Opposite: **Exquisite tile-work at the famous Shrine of Hazrat Ali in Mazari Shareef. Tilework dating from the Timurid period can be found in many mosques. The Timurid dynasty sparked a brilliant revival of artistic and intellectual life in Afghanistan and Central Asia in the 15th and early 16th century.**

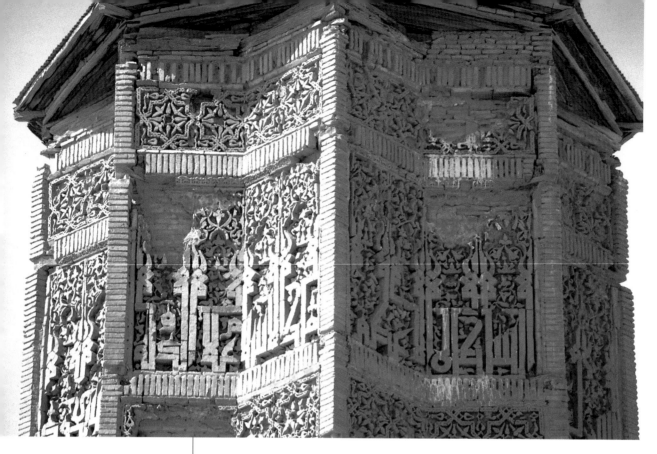

Above: **Intricate artwork on the Ghazni Victory Tower. The tower, which has survived almost a thousand years, was constructed during the reign of Mahmud of Ghazni (997–1030).**

Opposite: **The Friday Mosque in Herat. Parts of the mosque were damaged by bombing during the civil war.**

ISLAMIC HERITAGE

Afghanistan has played an important role in the development of Islamic culture in general. The greatest progress was made during the Ghaznavid era of the 10th and 11th centuries, and the Timurid era of the 14th and 15th centuries.

Mahmud of Ghazni summoned renowned men of learning to his court. Among those who came was Avicenna, a physician and philosopher. Avicenna is famous for his book *Canon of Medicine* which was used in medical schools in Europe before the 17th century. He also wrote many books on mathematics and astronomy. Also at Mahmud's court were 400 poets; among them was Firdausi, who composed the great epic *Shah Nama (Book of Kings)*. Mahmud and his successors also built magnificent mosques, palaces, and tombs.

The second great period of cultural development was at Herat under the Timurid rulers. Tamerlane and his successors ordered the construction of magnificent mosques and shrines. At Herat, Tamerlane established an elegant center of arts and learning.

ARCHITECTURE

Timurid architecture is characterized by its tall minarets, bulbous domes, and colorful tiles and is considered by scholars to be among the best in the world. Outstanding examples of such architecture found today include the Friday Mosque in Herat and the Blue Mosque at Mazari Shareef.

The Blue Mosque was built in 1420 by Amir Hussein and is said to contain the remains of Ali, the son-in-law of the Prophet Muhammad. The dome is of pristine simplicity, in sharp contrast to the lushly patterned walls. The architecture consists of sharp, clear forms, and the entrance is through great portals that lead into an extensive courtyard. The entire building is enhanced by contrasting forms and textures. To cover the walls, pieces of glazed tiles, in lapis lazuli, turquoise, deep green, yellow, black, and white, were carefully cut and fitted to form mosaic patterns of curving stems, leaves, and blossoms. Workmanship is so skilled that the panels appear to be painted, and the undulating surface causes the highly polished tiles to sparkle at certain angles.

Tile makers experienced in this ancient art still live in Afghanistan today and, in times of peace, have been employed in restoration works.

LITERATURE

Novels are rare in Afghan literature. Poetry, however, is highly revered and popular in Afghanistan, and each ethnic group has its own poetry, epics, and songs. These were usually transmitted orally from generation to generation, sometimes by performers who went from village to village entertaining the patrons of teahouses and *caravanserais*.

The most popular theme in Afghan literature is warfare, followed by love and jealousy, then religion and folklore. Most stories express a religious sentiment, besides extolling such virtues as courage.

Pushtun literature extols the warrior who dies for his principles. There are also many religious works in Pushtu, such as the *Makhzanul-Asrar* and the *Makhzanul-Islam*. Kushal Khan Khattak and Abdur Rahman, who lived in the 17th century, are the most important Pushtu poets. Kushal Khan Khattak is considered the national poet of Afghanistan. He also wrote books on philosophy, ethics, medicine, and an autobiography. He

THE TRAGIC TALE OF LEILA AND MAJNUN

The poignant romance of Leila, the daughter of a nomadic chief, and the poet Qais bin Amir, called Majnun—the name *Majnun* means "Mad One"—because his love cost him his sanity, has been told many times by poets, both as oral folklore and as literature. It is one of the most popular love stories, from Turkey all the way to the Malay archipelago in Southeast Asia.

In one version of the story, after Majnun has been driven mad by his love for Leila, his father approaches Leila's father to arrange a marriage between his son and Leila but is refused because Majnun is crazy. Leila ventures out in search of the wandering Majnun and is seen by Ibn Salam, a prince whom her father has committed her to marry. The prince imprisons Leila, but she escapes and finds Majnun. Realizing he cannot marry her because of his illness, Majnun sends his beloved back, and she dies in grief. A brokenhearted Majnun dies embracing her gravestone and is buried beside her.

CRITICIZING RELIGIOUS BIGOTRY

The knowing, the perceptive man
Is he who knows about himself,
For in self-knowledge and insight
Lies knowledge of the Holiest.
If in his heart there is no fear,
His deeds are not those of the good,
Pay no heed to one who's skilled
In quoting the Koran by heart.

— A poem by Kushal Khan Khattak

When Kushal Khan Khattak died in 1694, he left behind a considerable body of work, and many of his poems have since been translated by Pushtu scholars. Kushal Khan Khattak's grandson, Afdal Khan, later wrote a history of the Pushtuns.

is held in great awe by the Afghans as he was not only a great poet but also a warrior. Although constantly at war with the Moguls or with other Pushtuns, Khattak wrote great poetry about war, love, and life.

Baluchi poetry paints vivid pictures of the Baluchi countryside and way of life, and nature is a favorite theme. Generosity is exalted and greed condemned.

Turkic literature is shared by all its diverse groups. The magically swift horse, the faithful companion, and a hero possessing superhuman qualities are very common themes. Some of their epics that have become a shared heritage are the Uzbek *Alpamysh*, *Koblandy*, *Yer-Targyn*, and *Yedigy*, and the *Kyrgyz Manas*. The poem *Kudatkybilik* by Balasgun is held to be an outstanding example of Turkic literature. Balasgun's philosophy is said to be on par with that of Avicenna.

Persian literature is the most widely memorized and recited body of work throughout Afghanistan. It is well known to the educated Afghans, and their odes and ballads have been transmitted orally through the generations. Children are told tales from *Kalilah wa Dimnah*, a collection of animal stories very like Aesop's fables. Also popular are tragic love stories, similar to Shakespeare's *Romeo and Juliet*; the most famous of these being *Leila and Majnun*, *Adam and Durkhani*, *Farhad and Shirin*, and *Yusof and Zulekha*.

Contemporary prose and poetry are written in Dari and often imitate the classical Persian style and format. In 1947 a literary-political society called Awakening Youth was formed, and, for a time, there was a period of greater freedom of expression among authors.

An old painted wall in a teahouse in Kunduz. Afghan paintings often express a mood, rather than attempting realistic imagery.

VISUAL ARTS

Artists in Afghanistan were greatly influenced by the works of Behzad (mid-16th century), from the Timurid period in Herat. The Herat school of manuscript illumination developed a miniature style combining great technical skill with studied naturalism. Paintings consisted of precise and clear shapes in brilliant colors. Human, animal, and cloud forms were stylized, creating a tapestry-like effect.

No great sculptor or painter has emerged in Afghanistan since then, and of the graphic arts, only calligraphy and illumination have survived. This, however, has not been a profitable occupation since the introduction of printing.

An arts college, Maktabi Sanai, was established in the 1930s, where an annual exhibition was held; most of the works were oil paintings or watercolors. Two outstanding painters during the 1960s were Abdul Ghaffour Breshna and Khair Muhammad.

THEATER AND MOVIES

Original Persian plays, and those adapted from European classics or Arabic and Turkish comedies, are performed at the few theaters in Kabul, Herat, and Kandahar. Traveling companies take plays to the provincial towns and perform at local fairs.

Women's roles are often played by men, and most actors are amateurs. Among the European classics, the adaptations of Molière's comedies are very popular. Occasionally, Shakespeare's plays are also adapted.

Movie theaters usually show Indian movies, especially those in Hindi, and Pakistani movies.

A colorful wall painting of a mosque. Afghan art reached its peak in the 15th century when Herat became the center of a noted school of miniaturists, who illustrated poetical and historical works.

LEISURE

AFGHANS TAKE GAMES AND SPORTS very seriously. Winning in sports is, to the Afghan, of the utmost importance since a match is not just a friendly joust but is also a question of personal, tribal, and family honor.

Games are often held during festivals and celebrations and draw huge crowds of spectators. Kite flying is popular among Afghans.

CHILDHOOD GAMES

Childhood ends early in Afghanistan. Afghan children have few years in which to play as they are expected to help out with the chores. Their games are simple. Many are local variations of hide-and-seek and hopscotch. In rural Afghanistan a little girl's toy may be a crudely carved doll made by her father, and her brother may play with a slingshot. Children also play *boojoolibaazi*, a game resembling marbles but using sheep knucklebones.

Left: **Adult responsibilities begin early in Afghanistan. Household chores, such as washing up after a meal, must be completed before these children can run off to play.**

Opposite: **Afghan children playing soccer beside an ancient fort in Kabul. Soccer is one of the favorite sports in Afghanistan.**

A game of *buzkashi* in progress. *Buzkashi* is, by far, the most exciting Afghan national sport.

BUZKASHI

Buzkashi (BOOZ-kah-SHEE) is to Afghans what baseball is to Americans. The game is believed to have been developed in Central Asia and the plains of Mongolia. It plays a major role in the lives of the people of northern Afghanistan. For the farmer and the nomad, it serves as a reminder of a heroic ancestry. The game is often played by Afghans during the Now Roz (neh-ROHZ) festival in March. Only men participate in *buzkashi*.

Buzkashi literally means "grab the goat," but these days calves are more commonly used. The headless carcass of a calf is placed in the center of a circle formed by two teams of horsemen. Teams have been known to consist of as many as 1,000 players in unofficial games. When the signal is given, the riders move to the center, and each tries to lift the carcass onto his horse. This is no mean task in the noisy midst of flailing hooves, slashing whips, and the weight of the carcass. Horse and rider move in perfect harmony and are a joy to watch. Despite the potentially dangerous situation, serious injuries seldom occur as the horses are extremely well trained and their hooves never land on a fallen rider.

The Uzbeks, Tajiks, and Turkomans play buzkashi, *but the best players are the Uzbeks, who are acknowledged as the* buzkashi *champions of Afghanistan.*

112

Buzkashi

Once the calf is on his saddle, the rider secures the calf's legs under his own. He must then ride to a point one to three miles away, then return to the starting point and drop off the calf where he picked it up. Only then is he said to have scored a goal. During all this time, the other riders try to snatch the calf away from him.

The horses, ridden by the master players, or *chapandaz* (CHAP-an-DAAZ), who control the game, must be trained for at least five years.

Rules are laid down by the Afghan Olympic Federation, and two types of fouls have been introduced—hitting an opponent intentionally with one's whip and forcing him off his horse. Flagrant defiance of these rules means expulsion from the game, forcing the team to fall short by one man.

The rules also limit the duration of a game to an hour each with a 10-minute break at halftime. Official teams consist of no more than 10 players each. These rules are followed only at official games. *Buzkashi* played in Afghanistan, especially those in the north, is as full of thrills and spills as ever.

The current flag of Afghanistan has three vertical stripes of black, red, and green, and it was officially adopted on January 27, 2002. Above the emblem in the center of the flag is the inscription "There is no God but Allah, and Muhammad is His messenger." The emblem features a mosque with an arch that shows the direction of Mecca. This arch is called a mehrab *(MEH-rabb).*

THE AFGHAN HOUND

Afghan hounds are widely bred in Afghanistan and are used predominantly for hunting. They are known as *tazi* (TAWH-zee) and have shorter hair than their counterparts popular in the United States and Europe.

Despite their name, these hounds actually originated in Egypt thousands of years ago and became renowned only after being developed as hunters in the rugged terrain of Afghanistan.

Afghan hounds are highly valued by their owners for their hunting prowess. Afghans use the hounds to track down gazelles, goats, snow leopards, and bears. Marco Polo sheep and ducks are also popular game.

The Afghan hound weighs between 50 and 60 pounds (23 and 27 kg) and stands at a height of about 28 inches (71 cm).

Above: **Afghan boys practicing** *pahlwani.*

Opposite: **Afghan youths rest and chat happily outside a partially destroyed building. The fall of the Taliban marked the beginning of a new Afghan experience, one of hope and aspirations for the Afghan individual.**

PAHLWANI *AND OTHER SPORTS*

Most games native to Afghanistan are violent and vigorous. Wrestling, or *pahlwani* (pahl-wah-NEE), is popular with men all over the country. The rules are simple—the wrestler may grab the arms or the clothing of his opponent but must not touch his legs. Usually wrestlers seize their opponent's forearms and move sideways in a crablike, rocking motion, trying to catch their adversary off balance.

A man will leap high to try to toss his opponent, who in turn will twist in midair, ending behind the other man and holding him in a headlock. When one wrestler has been thrown to the ground and his shoulders pinned, the winner is lifted waist-high by his coach and carried around the field to the cheers of the jubilant crowd.

In Nuristan the men and boys play a game resembling rugby. The two teams each stand in a row, one row of players facing the other. One man from each team tries to dash past the opposing team, whose players try to block him. This body-shaking game consists of a great deal of pushing and tripping.

King Habibullah, during his reign from 1901 to 1919, introduced such Western sports as tennis, golf, and cricket, and built several golf courses in Afghanistan. After World War II other team sports were introduced. Their spirit of preserving honor enables the Afghans to excel at such games as basketball, soccer, volleyball, and field hockey.

MUSIC AND DANCING

The Afghan people love to sing and dance. In the evenings, young men get together to sing and to play music. Afghans sing even while they work or travel. Although musicians are not well respected, it is socially acceptable for Afghans to play music for their own entertainment. Performances of Indian music are well patronized in the cities. Before the Saur Revolution in 1978, the attitude toward women was more liberal, and Afghan singers such as Roxane and Sermand were popular.

The music of the mountains is purely Afghan: simple yet vigorous, resembling the flamenco music of Spain. In the cities the songs have a strong Indian influence and also often reflect Western trends.

Although different in many aspects, Afghan music is closer to Western music than to any other music in Asia. Their orchestra consists of a number of string instruments, drums, and a small hand-pumped harmonium.

Men dance at weddings and festivals. They usually dance with their swords and guns, in ever-widening circles. Older men form an inner circle, the younger men dance in the middle, and horsemen dance on the outside. The music starts on a slow beat and picks up tempo as the dance progresses, until music and dancers reach a frenzy. The music then stops abruptly. After a short break, the dancing and music begin again. During Pushtun weddings, men and women dance in rows of 10 to 12 people, each waving a brightly colored scarf above the head. Apart from weddings, women usually dance when no men are present.

Nuristanis play a form of field hockey using a stick with a cylindrical, bulbous head. This game is often played on rooftops 30 feet (9 m) high, and although the players seldom fall off, it can look very precarious to spectators.

FESTIVALS

AS IN MOST OTHER MUSLIM COUNTRIES, many holidays in Afghanistan celebrate important events in the Islamic calendar. These holidays are usually marked with special prayers and sermons in mosques. Many Afghans also take the opportunity to visit relatives or entertain with lavish meals. Independence Day in August and Revolution Day in April are the two most important secular holidays in Afghanistan.

EID AL-FITR

The most important month in the Islamic calendar is Ramazan, the ninth month, during which every Muslim, except the old, the sick, young children, and pregnant women, is required to refrain from food, drink, and tobacco from dawn to dusk.

Fasting during Ramazan is called *sawm*, or *rozah*, in Afghanistan. Before dawn Muslims eat a meal called the *sehri* and fasting begins at sunrise. Most Afghans break their daily fast by eating dates or raisins before their customary evening meal and tea. The observance of fasting is important and reflects the obedience of a believer of Allah. *Sawm* teaches self-control and abstinence or refrain from material wants.

Following the Islamic lunar calendar instead of the traditional Afghan solar calendar, Ramazan occurs 11 days earlier each year; fasting can be arduous when it falls in the summer. In 2005 Ramazan coincided with the months of October and November. During Ramazan, all activity slows down during the day, and the people liven up only after dusk falls.

The feast of Eid al-Fitr (EED AHL-fitr) commences after the month of fasting ends, on the first day of the month of *Shawal*. Celebrations usually last for three days. Congregational prayers are recited in mosques, after which Afghans visit their friends and relatives. New clothes, especially for the children, are made, and much food is prepared.

Opposite: **Here in the city of Mazari Shareef in Balkh, Afghans visit the Shrine of Hazrat Ali, also known as the Blue Mosque. Once again, mosques are active and bazaars come alive with activity and bright colors, and the people, despite the uncertain future ahead, go about making preparations for their much missed celebrations and festivities.**

Eid al-Fitr, pronounced as "EED ahl-fitr" in Arabic, is also known as Shaher-i-Bairam, pronounced as "shah-herh-REE-bai-RAHM," in Turkic, and Qamqai Akhta, pronounced as "kahm-kah-yee ekh-TAH," in Pushtu.

117

EID AL-ADHA

Once the fasting month and ensuing celebrations have ended, it is time for those planning to perform their obligatory pilgrimage to Mecca to start preparations for their journey. The hajj, or pilgrimage, takes place in the 12th month of the Muslim calendar, the rituals being performed in Mecca between the seventh and the 10th days. Those who have made the pilgrimage are referred to, respectfully, as *hajji* (HAW-jee), if male, and *hajjah* (HAW-jah), if female.

A feast known as Eid al-Adha (EED AHL-ad-ah) in the Muslim world is celebrated on the 10th day of the 12th month. Eid al-Adha is the Feast of the Sacrifice. Animals, such as sheep, goats, and camels, are sacrificed, especially by those who have already performed the hajj. This commemorates Abraham's faith, his obedience, and his love for Allah, and honors his willingness to offer his son as a sacrifice. Having passed the test of his faith, Abraham was stopped before the offering was made and at Allah's command a lamb was slayed and sacrificed instead.

One-third of the slaughtered animal is used by the family, another third is distributed to relatives, and the rest is given to the poor. This feast of the sacrifice is also referred to as Qurbaan (KOOR-bahn). In Turkic, it is known as Büyük Bairam (boo-yook bai-RAHM).

ASHURA

To the Shi'a, the most important religious period of the year is the first 10 days of the new year. This is a period of mourning, in memory of the killing of Hussein, the grandson of the Prophet Muhammad, at Karbala on October 10, 680, along with 72 of his immediate family and followers. The festival climaxes on the 10th day of the month of *Muharram* (MOO-har-ahm), called Ashura (ah-SHOO-rah).

Ashura is an optional fasting day. As the Shi'a population is relatively small, this day is celebrated on a more modest scale in Afghanistan than in countries with large Shi'a populations, such as neighboring Iran. Mourners in Iran, for example, join a procession through the streets, giving themselves over to frenzied expressions of grief, beating themselves, and sometimes even drawing blood.

BIRTH OF MUHAMMAD

Muslims also celebrate the birth of the Prophet Muhammad, who was born on the 12th day of the month of *Rabiul Awal* in 570. It is one of the most important holidays in Afghanistan, and prayers and feasting continue for weeks afterward. In homes, stories are told about Muhammad's life, his parents, and his birth. Religious leaders may also remind worshippers of their duties as Muslims.

The mosque is the focal point of most religious festivals. Besides the special congregational prayers conducted on these occasions, mosque officials organize the slaughter of animals and the distribution of meat during Eid al-Adha and the supervised collection of a tax from Muslims during Eid al-Fitr, as well as its subsequent distribution to the poor.

During Now Roz, friends and relatives visit one another, wishing everyone longevity, happiness, and productivity. Buzkashi *matches are held in Mazari Shareef and other towns. The spring festival of Now Roz is also celebrated on a grand scale in Iran.*

The prophet is believed to have died on his birthday, adding significance to the importance and solemnity of the feast.

NOW ROZ

Literally meaning a new day, Now Roz is the first day of spring and New Year's Day on the Afghan solar calendar. It falls on March 21. This festival dates back to the time when Zoroastrianism was still a powerful religion, long before Islam arrived in Afghanistan. Now Roz was once celebrated on June 21, or the solar equinox, but the date was later changed by the Achaemenids, the first royal dynasty of Persia, to the present date.

Several ancient superstitions are associated with the first day of the new year. For example, Afghans believe that on Now Roz, an ugly old woman called Ajuzak roams the world. If rain falls on that day, it is a sign that Ajuzak is washing her hair and the coming year's harvest will be bountiful. Infants are hidden to protect them from Ajuzak's evil eye.

During the celebrations, lavish meals are prepared in Afghan homes. Two dishes, *samanak* and *haftmehwah*, are especially cooked for the occasion. *Samanak*, a dessert made of wheat and sugar, can take more than two days to prepare. *Haftmehwah* consists of seven fruits and nuts to symbolize spring: walnuts, almonds, pistachios, red and green raisins, dried apricots, and a local fruit known as *sanjit*.

On Now Roz, the ceremonial raising of the flag at the tomb of Ali, Prophet Muhammad's son-in-law, is held at Mazari Shareef.

The standard of Ali is raised in the courtyard, and the devout touch the staff—a tradition known as *jandah bala kardan*—hoping to gain merit. The flagstaff remains standing for 40 days, during which thousands of pilgrims flock to Mazari Shareef, including the sick and crippled, hoping to be cured. Forty days after Now Roz, on the day the flag is lowered in Mazari Shareef, a distinctive red species of tulip blooms and then disappears soon after.

JESHN

One of the few holidays without religious significance in Afghanistan is Jeshn, or Independence Day. This is usually a weeklong celebration in August to mark Afghanistan's independence from the British in May 1919, after the Third Anglo-Afghan War.

Because the Treaty of Rawalpindi, which granted Afghanistan the freedom to conduct its own foreign affairs, was signed in August, and also because the harvest ends only in August, giving the rural population more freedom from work to participate in the festivities, celebrations are usually held at the end of August instead of May.

OTHER HOLIDAYS

Besides Independence Day and Revolution Day, Afghanistan observes Workers' Day, or Labor Day, which is also a national holiday in many other countries, on the first of May.

The national holiday of Revolution Day marks the date, April 27, 1978, on which President Daoud was overthrown. Besides the mandatory military parades and displays, buzkashi *matches are held and attended by huge crowds of spectators. All this happens during periods of peace, which have been rare for the war-torn country.*

NATIONAL HOLIDAYS OF AFGHANISTAN

First day of Ramazan	varies
Eid al-Fitr (end of Ramazan)	varies
Now Roz (New Year's Day)	March 21
Revolution Day	April 28
Workers' Day (Labor Day)	May 1
Eid al-Adha (Feast of the Sacrifice)	varies
Ashura (martyrdom of Hussein)	varies
Birth of Prophet Muhammad	varies
Jeshn (Independence Day)	August 19

FOOD

AFGHAN CUISINE IS A BLEND of the cooking styles of the many groups that invaded and occupied Afghanistan throughout the centuries. The strongest influences come from its neighbors Iran and India.

Both Iranian food, often regarded as the most refined of all Middle Eastern cuisines, and Indian food, probably the most sophisticated in South Asia, have had the advantage of thousands of years to develop and mature in terms of style and methods of preparations. Afghans have incorporated the best elements of the dishes of these ancient civilizations into their own delightful cuisine that is neither too spicy nor too bland. Its staples are rice and the bread called naan (nawn).

Left: **An enterprising young Afghan sells freshly prepared food. The Afghan diet excludes pork, which is forbidden by Islam.**

Opposite: **An Afghan teenager sells home-made bread in a bazaar in Kabul.**

Kabul street vendors with cartloads of naan for sale. Naan is also a favorite food in neighboring countries like Iran, Pakistan, and India.

NAAN

Naan is a flat bread that resembles oversized pancakes. It is made from every kind of grain that can be ground into flour, and even peas and mulberries. It is usually baked plain. Sometimes a filling, such as leeks or potatoes, is added for variety.

Naan is usually baked in a tandoor (tehn-DOOR), or clay oven, which is buried in the ground with hot coals under it; it can also be cooked on a hot, circular iron griddle.

The nomads often bake it on heated stones. Naan can be prepared in different shapes, too. Oblong is common, although in the north, oval naan is the norm.

This staple is especially important in the villages, where Afghans generally consume more bread than their counterparts in the towns. Town dwellers, who have access to a wider variety of food, consume larger amounts of rice and meat.

PILAU

Several varieties of rice are grown in the wetter areas of Afghanistan, including Kunduz, Jalalabad, and Laghman, and meals with rice are as common as those with naan. Rice may be served plain with side dishes, but on special occasions pilau (pah-LAO), also called pilaf, or *pilav* in Turkish, is served. Pilau is rice cooked with meats or vegetables. A guest at an Afghan's home is invariably invited to share a meal of pilau. Rural Afghans cook the rice with clarified butter (called ghee in Hindi), or lard from the tail of a fat-tailed sheep. Urban Afghans, however, are more likely to use vegetable shortening.

Pilau is a dish of tasty seasoned rice with meat and fresh vegetables.

Pilau is usually served with a side dish of vegetables and yogurt. Popular vegetables are squash, carrots, eggplant, spinach, potatoes, and peas. Sometimes pickled vegetables, called *toorshi*, are also served. In the cities of Kabul and Jalalabad a special hot chili sauce, *chutney-morch* (CHOOT-nee-moorch), is a favorite.

KEBAB

Kebabs are another favorite food of the Afghans. These are usually small cubes of meat skewered with onions, tomatoes, and pieces of fat, then grilled over open charcoal grills.

As with pilau, there are many different varieties of kebab. One of the most popular types is *kofta* (kohf-TAH) kebab, which is made with minced meat ground with onions. Another much-loved version is *shami* (SHAW-mee) kebab—minced meat mixed with beaten eggs and mashed potatoes before broiling.

Shorwa (shoor-WAH), a gravy usually made with mutton stock, is a favorite dish. Afghans dip their naan in it or drink it as a soup. In the north the Uzbek make their gravy with cattle blood and tomatoes.

Afghans usually have only two main meals a day, breakfast and dinner. Leftovers from dinner are often served for breakfast the following day.

PILAU GALORE!

The number of ways pilau may be cooked is limited only by the chef's imagination. The more popular varieties in Afghanistan are:

chilow (cheh-LAO): Plain rice with a large hunk of mutton or chicken buried within the mound of rice.

qaabili: Pilau with raisins, shredded carrot, almonds, and pistachios. A guest served *qaabili* pilau is held in great respect.

sabzi: Pilau with spinach

mushung: Pilau with small green peas

yakhni: Pilau with mutton in steamed rice

reshta: Pilau with eggs

baanjaani siyaa: Pilau with eggplant

morgh: Pilau with chicken

naranj (NAW-rehnj): Sweetish pilau with dried orange peel

kalapachah: Pilau with the head (including the animal's eyeballs) and feet of a sheep

landi (LOON-dee): Pilau with dried meat prepared like jerky; a favorite winter dish

OTHER FOODS

The Uzbek, Tajik, and other Afghans in the north enjoy pasta dishes, such as *ash* (awsh), a minestrone-type noodle soup. They also have several types of ravioli, called *ashak* (aw-SHAK), with a variety of fillings, from cheese to meat and leeks. A steamed meat dumpling, called *matoo*, similar to that found in Tibet, is eaten in the north, especially in the winter.

Dairy products are a staple of the Afghans' diet, especially in that of nomads and those in rural areas. Milk, not only from cows but also goats and sheep, is drunk. Besides milk and yogurt, many different types of cheese, both pasteurized and unpasteurized, are made and consumed.

Poultry, including chickens, ducks, turkeys, and guinea fowls, and eggs are also popular. Freshwater fish from Afghanistan's many rivers has become increasingly popular in recent years. In addition, game animals and small wild birds, a prized treat, are hunted and cooked.

Many of Afghanistan's sweets and desserts such as baklava and halvah are similar to those found in India and Pakistan. Besides these, both fresh and dry fruits are abundant. Fruits are of the Mediterranean and temperate variety and include melons, apples, pears, apricots, cherries, mulberries, and plums. Nuts, such as pistachios, almonds, and walnuts, are a major part of the Afghan diet and are often carried for quick snacks.

Rice is also cooked and served in several ways in addition to the pilau varieties. In convalescence, it is eaten with lentils as *kichri* (KEEK-ree) or

A fruit-and-vegetable seller in a market in Kandahar. Agricultural products made up about half of Afghanistan's exports in 2001. Nuts and fruits such as pistachios, almonds, grapes, mulberries, apricots, and pomegranates are the country's most important exports.

In Afghanistan, as in other Muslim countries, animals must be slaughtered according to prescribed Islamic rituals before their meat may be eaten.

Savoring a glass of hot tea in a teahouse in Kabul. Afghans often like their tea spiced with cardamom.

A favorite Afghan rice dish is dampok *(DAHM-pok), which is simply rice boiled with oil and water.*

shuleh (SHOO-lah), which is a gruel of rice and split green peas. This is usually served with a mixture of minced meat and ghee or sour cream.

A pudding called *faluda* (faw-loo-DAH) is prepared by steaming a mixture of wheat flour and milk in a porous bag for 10 to 12 hours. This is then pressed through a machine that makes spaghetti-like strings and served with syrup.

TEA

Tea is the national drink in Afghanistan and is extremely popular in a land where the consumption of alcohol is prohibited by Islam. It is served with meals and also is drunk in between meals.

128

HOSPITALITY AND ETIQUETTE AFGHAN STYLE

Hospitality is a very important aspect of Afghan culture. In an Afghan home a visitor will be offered the best that the family has, regardless of who the guest is. When one is invited to an Afghan home for tea, it is appropriate to bring a small gift. When invited for meals, one should bring sweets, fruits, or pastries. Gifts should preferably be nicely wrapped. The giver should be subtle and discreet when presenting a gift. Green wrapping paper is preferred for weddings.

A male visitor must offer his hand to the host. After shaking hands, the other hand should be placed on the heart and he should give a slight nod or bow. Physical contact between members of the opposite sex is forbidden, so it is not advisable to shake hands with the opposite gender.

Shoes should be removed before entering a house. Guests sit cross-legged on cushions and their feet should never point toward another person. The meal is served on plastic tablecloths spread on the floor. Food may be eaten from a common dish. The right hand is used for eating and serving. The left hand should never be used to eat, pass, or receive the food. A guest's plate is refilled as soon as it is empty. Out of politeness, some food should be left on the plate by the guest.

Guests are served snacks as well as tea, and their glasses of tea are constantly refilled. If a guest has had enough tea, he can cover his glass with his hand and say *bas*, meaning "enough."

Two types of tea are common in Afghanistan—black tea south of the Hindu Kush and green tea in the north. Both teas are served in teahouses found in towns and villages throughout the country, where Afghan men gather to drink tea and while away their leisure time.

Sugar is considered a luxury, and Afghans have to pay extra to sweeten their tea. Many Afghans soak a sugar cube in the tea, then either eat it or hold it to their mouth as they drink the tea. Unlike many other peoples in South Asia, most Afghans prefer their tea without any milk.

ASABIA EL AROOS (BRIDE'S FINGERS)

3 cups sugar
1½ cups water
Juice of 1 lemon
½ package (16 ounces, 455 grams) defrosted filo pastry
½ cup almond or pistachio pulverized in food processor with ⅓ cup sugar
¼ cup unsalted butter, melted
1 egg, lightly beaten

To make the syrup, boil about 2¾ cups of the sugar with the lemon juice and water for about 10 minutes or until the mixture is sticky and golden-brown. Preheat the oven to 375°F (190.6°C). Prepare one or two nonstick baking sheets. After cutting the filo pastry dough into half crosswise, and cutting these pieces again into halves, stack and cover the cut rectangular pieces of the pastry with a slightly damp towel to prevent the dough from drying.

Place two rectangular pieces of the cut dough on a clean and dry work surface. With the shorter side of the cut dough facing you, brush the dough lightly with melted butter and place a rounded tablespoonful of the pulverized nut mixture filling across it. Roll up the pastry dough from the shorter side to form a fat cigar-shaped cylinder. Do the same with the rest of the dough. Place the rolled pastry on the baking sheet with the cut edge facing down. Brush the top of the dough with the beaten egg and sprinkle some sugar over the rolls. Bake for 15 to 20 minutes until the dough turns golden brown, and then dip each cooked pastry into the hot sugar syrup. Serve them at room temperature.

MURGH (AFGHAN CHICKEN) KEBAB

2 large cloves garlic
½ teaspoon salt
2 cups plain whole milk yogurt
3 to 4 tablespoons pulp and juice of lemon
½ teaspoon cracked black pepper
2 pounds chicken breast, boneless

Place the salt in a wide shallow bowl and mash this together with the garlic to form a paste. When this is done, add the yogurt, lemon, and pepper to the garlic paste. After removing the skin and extra fat from the chicken meat, flatten it slightly. Next, coat the chicken in the yogurt mixture. Place the coated meat in a bowl and cover it. Leave the bowl in the refrigerator overnight.

Skewer the seasoned meat on sticks. Broil or grill the meat 6 inches from the heat for six to eight minutes on each side, or until done. Do not let the chicken breast char. Serve the chicken while it is hot. This recipe is sufficient for making 15 sticks of kebab.

MAP OF AFGHANISTAN

ECONOMIC AFGHANISTAN

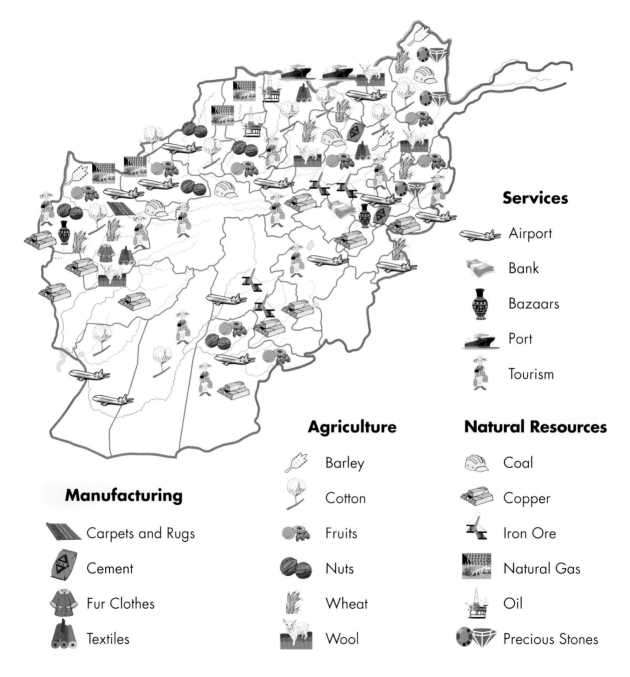

Services

- ✈ Airport
- 💵 Bank
- 🏺 Bazaars
- 🚢 Port
- 🧍 Tourism

Agriculture

- Barley
- Cotton
- Fruits
- Nuts
- Wheat
- Wool

Natural Resources

- Coal
- Copper
- Iron Ore
- Natural Gas
- Oil
- Precious Stones

Manufacturing

- Carpets and Rugs
- Cement
- Fur Clothes
- Textiles

ABOUT THE ECONOMY

OVERVIEW

After the fall of the Taliban regime, the international assistance of $2 billion in 2002, the recovery of the agricultural sector, and the reestablishment of market institutions in the country, the Afghan economy has improved significantly. Afghanistan is, however, still among the poorest countries of the world. Much of the population lacks the basic necessities of life. Most of its infrastructure needs to be reconstructed, and continued international aid, political stability, and peace are also vital for maintaining progress in Afghanistan. The cultivation of poppies and the opium trade, which account for as much as one-third of GDP, pose serious problems to the country.

GROSS DOMESTIC PRODUCT

$21.5 billion (2004 estimate)

GROWTH RATE

8 percent (2005 estimate)

LABOR FORCE

15 million (2004 estimate)

INFLATION RATE

16.3 percent (2005 estimate)

CURRENCY

USD1 = 45.55 Afghanis (2006)
1 Afghani = 100 puls

MAIN EXPORTS

Karakul sheepskins and wool, cotton, dried fruit and nuts, fresh fruit, natural gas

MAIN IMPORTS

Food, capital equipment, textiles, and petroleum products

AGRICULTURAL PRODUCTS

Wheat, fruits, nuts, opium, wool, mutton, and sheepskins

NATURAL RESOURCES

Natural gas, petroleum, coal, copper, chromite, talc, zinc, iron ore, salt, sulphur, and precious stones

POPULATION BELOW POVERTY LINE

56 percent (2005 estimate)

TELEPHONE LINES IN USE

33,100 (2002 estimate)

MOBILE PHONES

15,000 (2002 estimate)

INTERNET USERS

1,000 (2002 estimate)

TELEVISION STATIONS

At least ten: nine regional broadcast stations and one government-run station in Kabul

AIRPORTS

47 (2004 estimate):10 with paved runways, 37 with unpaved runways

CULTURAL AFGHANISTAN

Masjidi Jam
Located in Herat, this mosque is an example of the artistic sophistication of Ghorid art. The elaborate 12th century Jam Tower is located in its garden, and it is one of the world's finest Islamic buildings.

Mazari Shareef
Said to be the tomb of Hazrat Ali, the son-in-law and cousin of the Prophet Muhammad, this site is visited by thousands of people who come to celebrate Now Roz or the Afghan New Year.

Bamian
This village is the site of the two famed statues of Buddha, 155 feet and 174 feet (35 m and 53 m) tall, that were hewn into solid rock. They were destroyed by the Taliban but work is underway to reconstruct them.

Bandi Amir
This is the location of five beautiful clear blue lakes to the west of Bamian, formed by the flow of water over a succession of natural dams. It is the most outstanding site of the natural wonders of Afghanistan.

Gardens of Babur
These pleasant gardens were built by Emperor Babur in the 16th century. He died in Agra but asked to be buried here.

The Citadel
This ancient fort is claimed by some to have been built by Alexander the Great and is a reminder of the glorious period of kings, conquerors, and great pageantry, much like the fortress Bala Hissar of Kabul is.

Bazaars
The colorful and bustling bazaars in Kabul are places where Afghans shop and trade their wares. The ceaseless and uninhibited activity and bargaining, as well as the increasingly wide variety of goods traded, indicate the country's transition to democracy.

Bala Hisar (Kabul)
This fortress was the town's main defensive complex. It served as a residence for several rulers, including Babur and Tamerlane. It has figured in much of the country's history.

Kabul Museum
Kabul Museum, also known as the National Museum of Afghanistan, had the finest collection of antiquities in Asia. Much of it, unfortunately, has been looted or destroyed by the Taliban.

Museum of Islamic Art
This museum has a great collection of objects from the Ghaznavid period, such as mosaic tiles, glass, and bronze.

Shahri Zohak (The Red City)
Home to ruins of a cave city ravaged by Genghis Khan, this site is situated on a 350-foot (107-m) high cliff of red stone overlooking the Tagao Valley in Bamian. Due to the red color of the cliffs the city is situated on, it is also known as "The Red City."

The Mousallah Complex
The 15th century complex houses the remains of an old madrassa or religious school that is said to be the most beautiful model of the brilliant use of color in architecture. Destruction waged by British troops in the late 19th century and devastation caused by subsequent earthquakes have laid to ruins the 12 minarets that once stood tall in the complex.

Lashkargah
The capital of Helmand Province is the site of an ancient city built by Sultan Mahmood Ghaznawi. The ruins of the Masood Palace give an idea of the splendor of what was once the greatest empire of the east.

Shahri Gholgola (City of Noise)
This prosperous city from the 5th to the 7th centuries was laid to ruin by Genghis Khan. The "noise" refers to the screams that arose from the massacre.

The Minarets
These are the only two remaining minarets that were built in the 12th century. They inspired the Jam Tower, which in turn inspired the Qutub Minar of Delhi, India.

ABOUT THE CULTURE

OFFICIAL NAME
Islamic Republic of Afghanistan

NATIONAL FLAG
The flag consists of three bands—black, red, and green—and an emblem inscribed with the words "God is great" and "There is no God but Allah, and Muhammad is His messenger."

NATIONALITY
Afghan

CAPITAL
Kabul

AREA
250,000 square miles (647,500 square km)

POPULATION
31,057,000 million (July 2006 estimate)

PROVINCES
Badakhshan, Badghis, Baghlan, Balkh, Bamian, Farah, Faryab, Ghazni, Ghor, Helmand, Herat, Jowzjan, Kabul, Kandahar, Kapisa, Khowst, Konar, Kunduz, Laghman, Logar, Nangarhar, Nimroze, Nuristan, Paktia, Paktika, Parwan, Samangan, Sar-e-Pol, Takhar, Uruzgan, Wardak, Zabul

MAJOR CITIES
Kandahar, Mazari Shareef, Herat, Ghazni, Jalalabad, Farah, Shibarghan, Charikar, Kunduz, Maimanah, Puli Khumri

MAJOR RIVERS
Helmand, Amu Dar'ya, Harirud, Kabul

OFFICIAL LANGUAGES
Pashtu and Dari (Afghan Persian)

ETHNIC GROUPS
Pashtun 42 percent; Tajik 27 percent; Hazara 9 percent; Uzbek 4 percent; Aimak 4 percent; Turkmen 3 percent; Baloch 2 percent; and others

MAJOR RELIGIONS
Islam: Sunni Muslims, Shi'a Muslims

FERTILITY RATE
6.7 children per woman (2006 estimate)

BIRTH RATE
46.6 births per 1,000 Afghans (2006 estimate)

INFANT MORTALITY RATE
160 deaths per 1,000 Afghan births (2006 estimate)

DEATH RATE
20.34 deaths per 1,000 Afghans (2006 estimate)

LIFE EXPECTANCY
42.3 years male; 42.7 years female

LITERACY RATE
Total population 36 percent; male 51 percent; female 19.6 percent (2005 estimates)

TIME LINE

IN AFGHANISTAN	IN THE WORLD

328 B.C.
Alexander the Great captures Bactria (now Balkh).

753 B.C.
Rome is founded.

116–17 B.C.
The Roman empire reaches its greatest extent, under Emperor Trajan (98–17).

A.D. 642
The Arabs introduce Islam to Afghanistan.

A.D. 600
Height of Mayan civilization

998–1030
Mahmud of Ghazni turns Ghazni into a great cultural center as well as a base for forays into India.

1000
The Chinese perfect gunpowder and begin to use it in warfare.

1370
Afghanistan is incorporated into the vast empire of Tamerlane, whose Timurid dynasty ends after 100 years. Their capital is at Herat. This is a prosperous period for Afghanistan.

1500s
Babur, a descendant of Tamerlane and the founder of India's Mogul dynasty, moves the capital to Kabul.

1530
Beginning of trans-Atlantic slave trade organized by the Portuguese in Africa.

1558–1603
Reign of Elizabeth I of England

1620
Pilgrims sail the Mayflower to America.

1747
Ahmad Shah Durrani (born Ahmad Khan Abdali) creates a single Afghanistan.

1776
U.S. Declaration of Independence

1789–99
The French Revolution

1838–42
The First Anglo-Afghan War is waged.

1861
The U.S. Civil War begins.

1869
The Suez Canal is opened.

1878–80
The Second Anglo-Afghan War breaks out.

1914
World War I begins.

1919
Amanullah comes into power and launches the third Anglo-Afghan War to gain complete independence from the British. August 19 is celebrated as Afghanistan's Independence Day.

IN AFGHANISTAN	IN THE WORLD
1919–29 King Amanullah introduces reforms for modernization and secularism. Amanullah abdicates in early 1929. Kabul falls to forces of Habibullah, also called Bacheh Saqow, a Tajik brigade. Mohammad Nadir Khan, also known as Nadir Shah, a cousin of Amanullah, later defeats Bacheh Saqow in October and is declared king. **1933** Mohammad Nadir Khan, or Nadir Shah, is assassinated by a Kabul student. **1933–73** Zahir Shah rules.	
	1939 World War II begins. **1945** The United States drops atomic bombs on Hiroshima and Nagasaki. **1949** The North Atlantic Treaty Organization (NATO) is formed. **1957** The Russians launch Sputnik. **1966–69** The Chinese Cultural Revolution
1973 Former prime minister Mohammed Daud Khan seizes power in a military coup and declares a republic, headed by himself. **1978** A bloody coup by the People's Democratic Party of Afghanistan breaks out. Daud and his family are killed. Nur Mohammed Taraki becomes the prime minister. **1979** After a shoot-out in the palace, Hafizullah Amin takes over from Taraki, who is killed. The Soviet Union invades Afghanistan. Hafizullah is killed, and Babrak Karmal is installed as president. The Muslim groups unite to form the *mujahidin* (guerrilla warriors) and launch resistance to the Soviet invasion.	

TIME LINE

IN AFGHANISTAN	IN THE WORLD

1986
Karmal is replaced by Najibullah.

1986
Nuclear power disaster at Chernobyl in Ukraine

1988
A cease-fire is declared. The Geneva Accord is signed, and the governments of Pakistan and Afghanistan are guaranteed noninterference from the United States and the USSR.

1989
Full withdrawal of Russian forces in Afghanistan by mid-February.

1991
Break-up of the Soviet Union

1992
The Communist regime of Najibullah is overthrown by the *mujahidin*. Civil war erupts with the various militia fighting among themselves.

1994–98
The Taliban captures Kandahar and Kabul and, by 1998, occupies 90 percent of the country. The al-Qaeda bombs U.S. embassies in Nairobi (Kenya) and in Dar-es-Salaam (Tanzania).

1997
Hong Kong is returned to China.

2001
In October the United States launches a retaliatory military campaign in Afghanistan after the September 11 terrorist attacks, and the Taliban government is ousted from Kabul by November. The Bonn Agreement is signed in December.

2001
Terrorists crash planes in New York, Washington, D.C., and Pennsylvania.

2003
War in Iraq

OCTOBER 2004
A democratic presidential election is conducted. Hamid Karzai emerges as clear victor and is Afghanistan's first elected president after more than two decades of conflict in the war-torn country.

2005
General elections are held in September. Results of landmark parliamentary elections are finalized by November, and in December the National Assembly is inaugurated.

GLOSSARY

Azan
The call to prayer.

baadi sadu beest roz
These strong winds along the Iran-Afghanistan border are also known as the "Wind of One Hundred and Twenty Days."

buzkashi (BOOZ-kah-SHEE)
Game in which teams of horsemen compete to carry a headless calf over a goal line.

chadari (chawdari)
Traditional garment that is worn in public and covers a woman from head to foot.

hajj (HAHJ)
Pilgrimage to Mecca.

jangal (jehng-EHL)
Forest or wooded area.

jihad (jee-HAHD)
The permanent struggle to make the word of Allah supreme.

jooyi (joo-YEE)
Artificially made pools or streams.

Loya Jirga (law-yah jorhr-GAH)
The Great Council in which Afghan elders gather to discuss national issues.

Meli Shura (MEH-li-SHOO-rah)
Highest legislative body of Afghanistan.

mujahidin (moo-JAH-hee-DEEN)
"Holy warriors" of Islam or Muslim guerrilla fighters.

mullah (mool-LAH)
Muslim teacher or scholar.

pahlwani (pahl-wah-NEE)
Wrestling.

pilau (pah-LAO)
Rice cooked with meats or vegetables.

posteen (poss-TEEN)
A coat made of sheepskin.

purdah (perhr-DAH)
Seclusion of Muslim women.

Pushtoonwali (PUHSH-toon-WAH-lee)
Code of conduct upheld by Afghans.

Salat (saw-LAWT)
Prayers.

Shahadat (sheh-hah-DEHT)
The belief in Allah as the only God, and in the Prophet Mohammed as His messenger.

tandoor (tehn-DOOR)
A traditional clay oven used to bake naan and other foods

Wolesi Jirga (woo-LAW-si jorhr-GA)
House of the People, or House of Representatives.

yurt (yerht)
A portable tent used by seminomads. It can be set up and dismantled with much ease and speed.

zakat (zeh-KAHT)
Alms given to the poor every year.

FURTHER INFORMATION

BOOKS

Ellis, Deborah. *Parvana's Journey*. Toronto: Groundwood Books, 2003.
———. *The Breadwinner*. Toronto: Groundwood Books, 2001.
Khan, Rukhsana. *Roses in My Carpet*. Markham: Fitzhenrry and Whiteside, 1998.
Staples, Suzanne Fisher. *Under the Persimmon Tree*. New York: Farrar Straus and Giroux (Books for Young Readers), 2005.

FILMS

Afghanistan Revealed: The Untold Story of a Land and its People. National Geographic, 2001.
Afghanistan: The Lost Truth. Directed by Malek Nassar, 2003.
Beneath the Borqa in Afghanistan. Caipirinha Productions, 2001.

MUSIC

Afghanistan. Playasound Air Mail Music, 2000.
Afghan Untouched by various artists. Traditional Crossroads, 2003.
The Silk Road: A Musical Caravan by various artists. Smithsonian Folkways, 2002.

BIBLIOGRAPHY

Afghanistan in Pictures. Minneapolis, MN: Lerner Publications, 1989.
Ansary, Mir T. *Afghanistan: Fighting for Freedom*. New York: Macmillan Children's Book Group, 1991.
Clifford, Mary L. *The Land and People of Afghanistan*. New York: Harper Collins Children's Books, 1989.
Herda, D. J. *Afghan Rebels*. New York: Franklin Watts, 1990.
Kazem, Halima. *Countries of the World: Afghainstan*. Milwaukee, WI: Gareth Stevens Publishing, 2003.
Michael, Roland, and Michaud, Sabrina. *Afghanistan*. New York: Thames and Hudson, 1990.
Afghanistan Business Culture and Etiquette. www.kwintessential.co.uk
Afghanistan Online. www.afghan-web.com
Afghanistan's Environmental Casualties. www.motherjones.com
BBC: History of Afghanistan. www.bbc.co.uk
CIA: The World Fact Book—Afghanistan. www.cia.gov/cia/publications/factbook
CIC Wildlife. www.cic-wildlife.org
NationMaster.com—Encyclopedia. www.nationmaster.com
Kabul Museum. http://portal.unesco.org

INDEX